HART ♥ MOTORS

Since 1937

Founded by E.P. "Jeff" Hart in 1937, Hart Motors celebrates a long-standing tradition of service in Salem. A true family enterprise, Hart's son and three grandsons work with the company today - and still offer the same superior service that has kept customers coming back for sixty-five years.

Where it all began - Hart Motors' first shop near the corner of Main and Broad, 1937-1945.

ANNOUNCING---

THE OPENING

HART MOTOR COMPANY

FORMERLY F. W. WHITESCARVER, INC.

FRIDAY, OCTOBER 1, 1937

IN NEW AND LARGER QUARTERS IN THE SNYDER BUILDING CORNER MAIN AND BROAD STREETS

OLDSMOBILE

SALES and SERVICE

NEW 1938 CARS NOW ON DISPLAY

COMPLETE SERVICE FOR ALL CARS
SPECIAL GREASING EQUIPMENT

HART MOTOR COMPANY

SNYDER BUILDING

BROAD AND MAIN STS.

SALEM, VIRGINIA

PHONE 300

The Hart Motors staff in 1954, with Jeff Hart standing in the doorway of their new headquarters on the southwest corner of Main and Strawberry Alley (across from today's Roanoke County courthouse). The business operated in this building, the site of a 19th century livery stable, from 1945 to 1973.

Saturn of Roanoke Valley
Saturn of Lynchburg

VALUE RATED USED CARS

Hart Motors today, where putting the customer first is a family tradition.

Hart Motors • 1431 East Main Street, Salem • Phone: 444-4444

A Town by the Name of Salem

The Past in Pictures

John D. Long
Mary Crockett Hill

A bicentennial publication of the
Salem Museum and Historical Society

Design and Photo Editing:
Pamela C. Helm

Scanning and Digital Photography:
Bron Duncan

Printing: R.R. Donnelley

Cover Painting: Harriett Stokes

Send inquiries to:

Salem Museum & Historical Society
801 East Main Street
Salem, Virginia 24153
www.salemmuseum.org
info@salemmuseum.org

First edition: October, 2002

ISBN 0-9724674-0-8

Corporate Sponsors

Salem Museum Bicentennial Founder's Circle

HART ❤ MOTORS

RR DONNELLEY

TOTALLY DIGITAL

P.C. HELM

Salem Museum Bicentennial Pioneer's Circle

Carter Machinery, Inc.

Salem Museum Bicentennial Patron's Circle

First Virginia Bank, Southwest

FNB/Salem Bank & Trust

Graham-White Mfg.

Hampton Inn ~ Salem

The Inn at Burwell Place

Just Financial Planning

Edward Lautenschlager

Marizel's Flowers

Salem Times-Register

Smith & Co., Accountants

City of Salem Bicentennial Sponsors

R.M. JOHNSON & SONS
JEWELERS

Photo by Dr. Harry Minarik.

2002 Reunion of Presidents of the Salem Historical Society. Clockwise from seated: Woody Middleton, Judy Goodwin, Guy Ritter, Jim Fulghum, John Hildebrand, David Foster, David Robbins, Temp Norris, Mike Maxey, Inez Good; middle, front to back: Lon Savage, Warren Moorman, Mark Miller. (Peggy Shenberger not pictured.)

Salem Historical Society Board Members

** denotes served as president*

Sara Ahalt
Mildred Andrews
Eugene Bane
Jeanne Becker
Leonard Becker *
Anne Stuart Beckett
Barbara Bell
Ervin Brooks
Barbara Brown
Maxwell Brown
Dorothy Burke
Katherine Burke
Nona Bush
Dorothy Butler
Ray Byrd
Clarence Caldwell
Emily Paine Carter
Mildred Chapman
Page Chapman
W. Frank Chapman
Karen Chewning
Samuel R. Crockett *
H.C. Crotts
Paul Curran
Harriett Darst
Lellen Dawson

Peyton B. Douglas *
May Duncan
Charles H. Fisher
Frances Fitzgerald
David L. Foster *
Joyce Foster
James H. Fulghum Jr.*
Helen Garbett *
Vernon Garbett
Christopher Gladden
Nancy Gladden
Inez Good *
Judy Goodwin *
Robert Goodwin III
Max Green
Carolyn Greene
Marylen Harmon
Martha Higginbotham
John Hildebrand *
Pat Hooker
Robert Hunt
Alfred D. Hurt*
Helen Johnson

Mary Johnson
Dan Joiner
Jennifer Joiner
Jane Kelly
Joseph LaRocco
Hugh Lee
Roy Lochner
Michael C. Maxey *
Joseph McCarthy
Anna McClung
Norwood Middleton*
Mark Miller *
Nancy Miller
Judy Minahan
Clarence Mitchell
Warren L. Moorman*
James Nininger
Temp Norris *
Barbara Oetgen
Laurie Peery
Alice Peters
Iris Peterson
R.W. Peterson Jr.

Jenny Powell
Jenny Proctor
Donald Reid
Guy A. Ritter *
Frankie Robbins
J. David Robbins *
Robert St. Lawrence
Robert Saul
Lon Savage *
Merriman Sears
Peggy Shenberger *
Betty Sherrard
Buck Simmons
Lucile Snow
Robert Stauffer
Evelyn Bondurant Taney
James Taney
Joseph C. Thomas
Betty Waldron
Margaret Watts
Emma Webber
William G. Wells *
Lillian Whitescarver
William E. Whitesell Jr.
Jean Woltz
Max Woltz
James P. Woods Jr.

Acknowledgements

Two names appear on the cover of this book—there should be dozens.

Most egregiously missing are the names Pam Helm and Bron Duncan. Pam, our designer, endured countless revisions, finicky edits, and missed deadlines, yet consistently produced excellent and efficient work—and did so cheerfully. Bron, our scanning wizard, accomplished miracles, maneuvering through piles of old photos, dusty slides, and delicate artifacts with the greatest of ease. We knew we had found the right people for the job from our very first conversations: "I'm good under pressure," said Pam; "Sure, I can scan anything," said Bron.

John Pecaric, Donal Robb, Cherie Coleman and Eric Rishell of R.R. Donnelley were extremely charitable with their resources, patience, and expertise.

From the beginning, this Bicentennial publication was championed by Teri Atkins, Salem's special events coordinator. We are grateful as well for the generous support of Mayor Sonny Tarpley; Vice Mayor Alex Brown; councilmen John Givens, Gerald Pace, and Howard Packett; City Manager Forest Jones; Parks and Recreation Director Charlie Hammersley; Public Information Officer Melinda Payne; and (the folks who *really* run the city) Joyce Bailey and Krystal Coleman.

Emily Carter and Sara Ahalt were efficient and beneficial copy editors. Museum staff Pauline Batten, Helen Johnson, and Christina Smith worked through tedious but necessary details; likewise college interns Kass Bratton, Charlene Mullins, Bob Rodgers and Jared Poff.

Mark and Linda Miller, of Roanoke College's History Department and Archives respectively, provided advice as well as material. Aaron Cook's Eagle Scout project of copying historic photographs for our use made a significant contribution to this book. Thanks also to Teena Cook, his mom. Ron Bell and Belinda Harris of the *Roanoke Times* graciously let us peruse and use their archives. Ditto Kent Chrisman of the History Museum of Western Virginia. Joey Moldenhauer of the Archeological Society of Virginia offered both assistance and sound advice. Ray Robinson and Jim Morgan of the *Salem Times-Register* made materials available; as did sports writer and photographer Brian Hoffman. The Electric, Police, Fire and Street Departments supplied interesting images of key moments in the city's development. Harriett Stoke's lovely painting of Salem, commissioned by the Salem Fine Arts Commission and presented to City Council for the Bicentennial, graces the cover of the book. Harry Minarik loaned us his talents behind a camera when needed. Frankie and David Robbins' organizational skills were invaluable and inspirational. And finally, Salem Historical Society President Michael Maxey and the Board of Directors supported the project from cover to cover.

Appreciation is also due to those who offered photos to this project. These contributions were fascinating, and had space not been an issue, we would have used them all. Many photos seen here, however, were donated to the Historical Society long before this book was conceived. While we don't have room to list all of these generous contributors, a few deserve special mention: Betsy Barker, Dorothy Butler, Helen Cobbs, Chris Gladden, Sydney Hunter, Asbury Maury, and Wes McCarty. The late Frances Fitzgerald, Louise Hurt, and Ted Webber also gave generously in past years. Postcard collectors George Wade and Bob Stauffer were invaluable resources, as was Warren Moorman, who spent decades copying images and documenting events for the Salem Historical Society. Copies of Temp Norris' family photos were especially helpful. Peter Ostaseski of Poindexter-Bolt Advertising donated a treasure trove of images from Lakeside Amusement Park.

Stewart Hill and Candy Daugherty were terrific (and terrifically patient) sounding boards. While two-year-old Isabelle Hill may not remember this project, Mom will not soon forget her patience throughout.

These acknowledgements would be incomplete without a grateful tribute to Norwood C. Middleton. His 1986 *Salem: A Virginia Chronicle* is the foundation for this book, and anyone with an interest in local history owes him thanks and respect. Our pictorial history attempts to complement, not supplant, his monumental tome. If you have bought this book and don't yet own a "Woody," head over to the Salem Museum right now and pick up the rest of the story.

Table of Contents

1

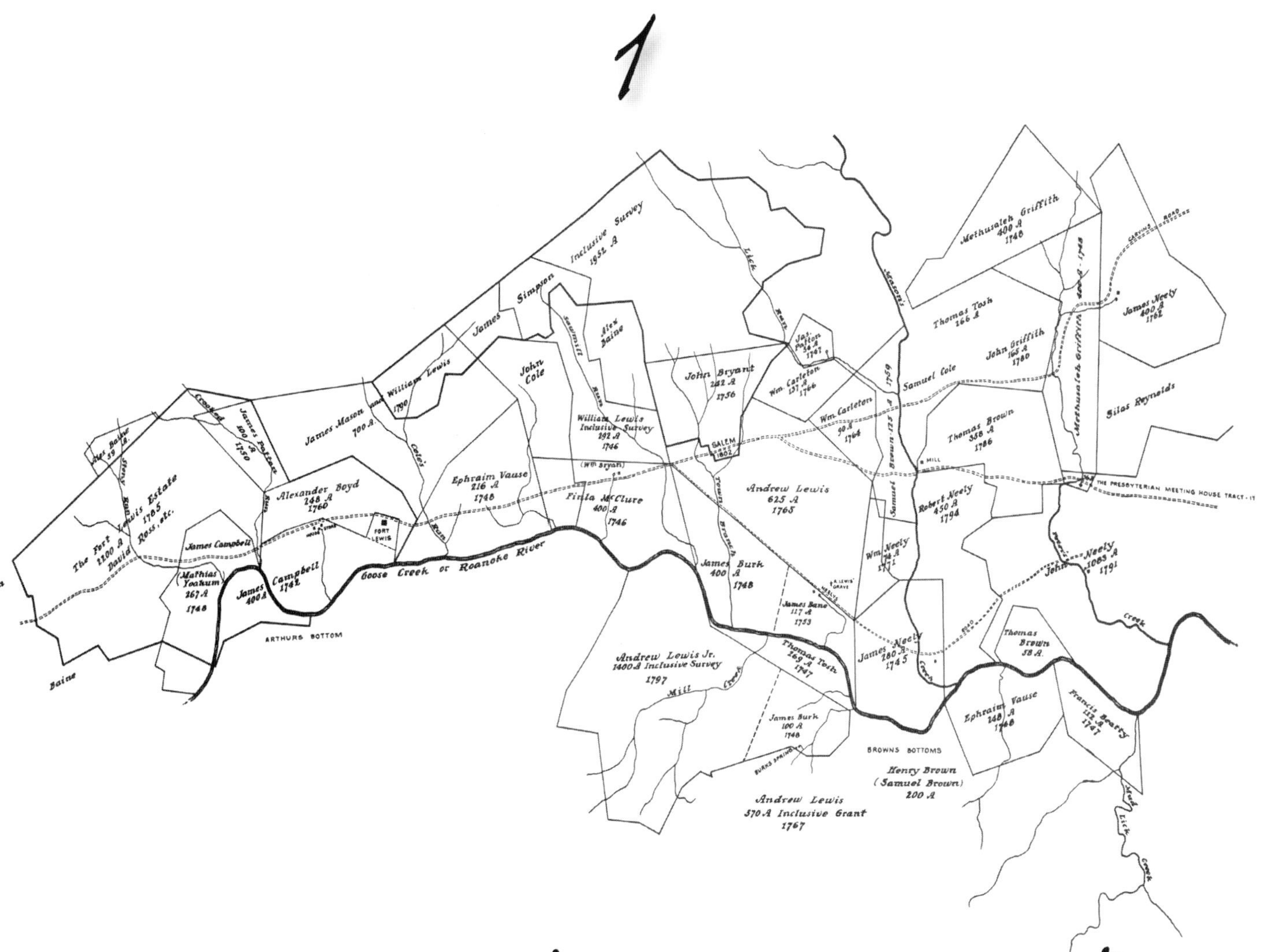

Life on the Roan Oak

Before 1802

Chapter 1

Previous page: Map of early Roanoke Valley settlements from Kegley's Virginia Frontier.

Trigger from a 17th century British firearm called a snaphaunce, found in the Graham-White archeological dig. Such trade artifacts establish European contact with the Indians living in the Roanoke Valley.

Center: Clay pipes, stone projectile points, and other artifacts found at the Graham-White site.

There was no Salem before 1802, but there was history here—as certain and tangible as the ground beneath our feet. In fact, it is to this very ground that we look for clues of Salem's first people.

The earliest residents of the Roanoke (or "Roan Oak") Valley were, of course, Native Americans. Long before (perhaps 10,000 years before) European settlers filtered into this region, generations of Indians lived and died here. Since no record exists to describe their culture firsthand, we must depend primarily on archeological evidence—quite literally what lies underground—to help us understand their ways.

In the 1990s, excavations at the Moyer Sports Complex (or Graham-White site) revealed numerous Native American artifacts, including countless beads, shells, projectile points, clay pipe pieces, a handful of metal fragments and—perhaps the most revealing find—a three-inch trigger from a 17th century English firearm. In total, these artifacts suggest that an active village of Indians made the riverside their home prior to and during the period of early contact with European settlers.

One of the features excavated at the Graham-White site.

While we may never know for certain the exact identity of these Native people, there may be further clues in the 17th century diary of the explorer Robert Fallam, who with Thomas Batts passed through this area in 1671. His account of September 9, 1671, details the explorers' entrance into what may well have been Salem:

(W)e came to a very steep descent, at the foot whereof stood the Tetera (sic) Town in a very rich swamp between a branch and the main river of Roanoke circled about with mountains. We got thither about 3 o'clock after we had traveled about twenty-five miles. Here we were exceedingly civilly entertained.

The exact location of "Tetera Town" has remained a matter of conjecture for generations. Proposed sites have ranged from Roanoke to Radford, but most scholars contend that it was in the Roanoke Valley; the Graham-White excavation and the topography at that site make Salem a prime candidate.

Reconstructed clay vessel uncovered during the Graham-White dig.

Whether or not the Native Americans near the river in Salem were the same as those who so "civilly entertained" Batts and Fallam, they almost certainly belonged to the same tribe. Related to the Siouan people, the Toteras were known to live a relatively peaceful, semi-nomadic life in western Virginia's river valleys, where natural resources were abundant enough to make life sustainable. They did not remain in the area long after initial European contact, however. Devastated by diseases such as smallpox and harassed by hostile Iroquois from the north, the Toteras relocated to the border between Virginia and North Carolina, and from there eventually moved to Pennsylvania and Canada. Thus, the Roanoke Valley was virtually unpopulated when white settlers began to arrive and claim homesteads in the late 1730s.

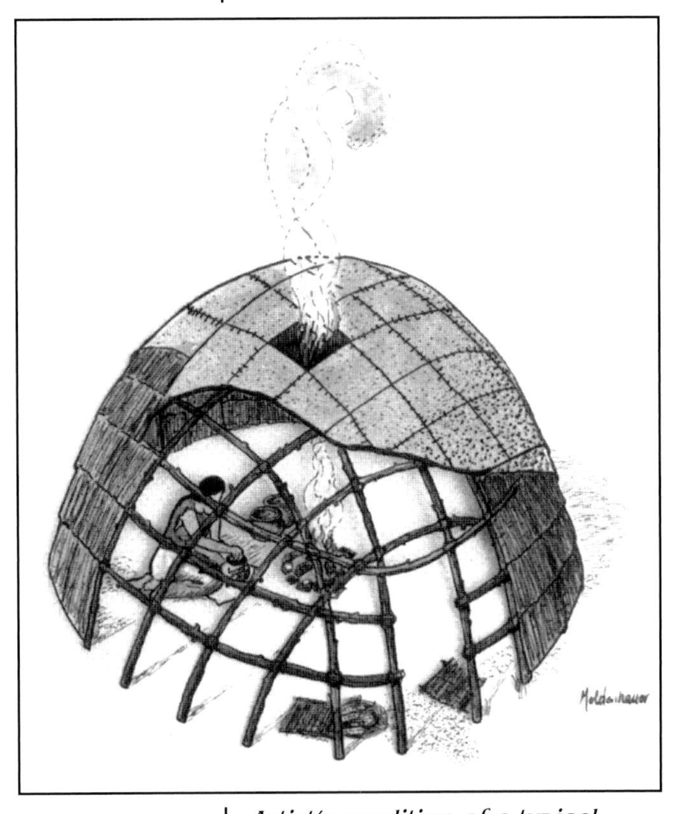

Artist's rendition of a typical Eastern Woodlands wigwam, such as Batts and Fallam may have visited.

In the middle to late 18th century, we find upwards of twenty families owning estates in the general area of today's Salem. Life for these settlers was hard. Struggling against the elements was a daily chore that led to occasional tragedy, as in 1749 when a major flood killed Peter Kinder, who lived along the creek that would bear his first name. Additionally, the threat of Indian attack was a serious concern—with notorious raids in nearby communities creating justifiable fear in frontier families. A fort was built in the late 1750s on the estate of Captain James Campbell (just

Lewis ~~& him~~ and shewed it to him: Lewis, indignant at such a scandalous,
and unjust representation, accused Grant of his Duplicity in the
Presence of the French Officers, and challenged him; but Grant pruden-
ly declined the Combat, after receiving the grossest Insults, by spitting in
his Face, and degrading Language.

After the French had blown up the Fort and departed for Quebeck with the
prisoners, in going up the Alleghany-River, it was very cold, and Grant lay
shivering in the Boat cursing the Americans and their Country, threatening, if
ever he returned to England he would let his Majesty know their Insignificance,
and the Impropriety of the Trouble and Expense of the Nation, in endeav-
ouring to protect such a vile Country and People, for this provoking language, Genl. Lewis did chide him severely. — Genl. Lewis was, in Person, upwards of six Feet high, of uncommon Strength and Agility, and his Form
of the most exact Symmetry that I ever beheld in Human Being, had
stern and invincible Countenance, of a distant and reserved Deportment
which rendered his Presence more awful than engaging. He was a
Commissioner with Dr Thomas Walker, to hold a treaty on Behalf of the
Colony of Virginia, with the six Nations of Indians, together with the Commis-
sioners from Pennsylvania, New-York, and other eastern provinces,
held at Fort Stanwix, in the Province of Newyork, in the year 1768. it was
there remarked by the Governour of Newyork, that the Earth seemed to
tremble under him as he walked along. His independent Spirit de-
spised Sycophant Means of gaining Popularity, which never rendered more than
his superior Merits extolled. Such a Character was not calculated to
gain much Applause by commanding an Army of Volunteers, without
Discipline, Experience, or Gratitu[illegible] many took Umbrage: because they were
compelled to do their Duty; and others thought the Duties of a common
Soldier, were beneath the Dignity of a Volunteer, every one found some
imaginary Complaint. When Congress determined to be independent, and appointed General officers to command our Armies to prosecute the War, for
Independence, and defending our Liberty, they nominated Genl Washing

Page from John Stuart's account of the Battle of Point Pleasant. Stuart, an officer under Andrew Lewis, wrote this memoir in 1820. Notice the remark by the Governor of New York that "the Earth seemed to tremble under (Lewis) as he walked along."

west of modern-day Salem) to serve as a first line of defense and a safe haven for families during times of attack.

The Salem fort was named to honor one of the Valley's most notable soldiers and patriots, Andrew Lewis (1720-1781). When a malicious landlord murdered a family member, Andrew Lewis' father retaliated by killing the landlord. Forced to flee Ireland, the family sailed to America. The Lewises settled in the Shenandoah River Valley of Augusta County and soon became a leading family on the frontier. Life on the western lands necessitated learning to defend one's home, and so young Andrew was reared to be a soldier. In the French and Indian War he fought alongside George Washington and was briefly held prisoner in Canada.

About 1767, Lewis moved with his wife and children to Richfield, an estate of 625 acres that included a good bit of what would become Salem. While the precise location of the Lewis home has never been determined beyond doubt, it is understood to have been in the vicinity of today's Salem Civic Center. Lewis was considered the most experienced soldier in Virginia besides Washington, and hence was chosen by the royal Governor Lord Dunmore to lead an expedition against the Shawnees in the autumn of 1774. Shawnee Chief Cornstalk had been leading raids against the western settlements, and Dunmore was determined to end the incursions. He instructed Lewis to assemble a force of frontier militia, about a thousand strong, and meet the governor's British Regulars at Point Pleasant on the Ohio River. Lewis complied, but, while waiting for Dunmore's reinforcements, was attacked by Cornstalk's forces. After a pitched battle lasting the day, Cornstalk retreated across the Ohio, never again to threaten the Virginia frontier. Lewis lost about 45 officers and men, including his brother Charles. A good friend and neighbor, Dr. William Fleming, was seriously wounded.

General Andrew Lewis at the epic Battle of Gwynn's Island where he evicted from Virginia the last British royal governor. The painting above and the statue below are works of artist Anne Bell and were placed in 2000 at the Salem Civic Center, on land once owned by Lewis.

The Battle of Point Pleasant was a crucial, though often under-appreciated, event in American history. By ousting the last hostile Indians from the frontier, Lewis had pacified the Ohio River Valley, a fact that would be of immense value in the coming Revolution, since Virginia's soldiers could then concentrate on defeating the British. Furthermore, many have argued that resentment towards the British for failing to arrive at the battle on

The silhouette above is the only surviving image of Andrew Lewis created during his lifetime. Any other portraits of the General likely perished when his home, Richfield, burned several years after his death.

time helped expand the growing rift between Virginians and their mother country. As such, Point Pleasant has sometimes been termed the first battle of the Revolution.

Andrew Lewis' military exploits did not end at Point Pleasant. In July 1776, mere days after the thirteen colonies had declared their independence, Lewis led a force against Lord Dunmore at Gwynn's Island near Williamsburg. Dunmore fled with his armada. Thus, Lewis took credit for chasing out of Virginia the last hostile Indians and the last British Governor.

Had Lewis lived to see his beloved Virginia gain her independence with victory over the British, he might have become one of her most illustrious leaders, along with his friends Washington, Jefferson, Madison, and Henry. However, he died of a fever in the last year of the war, only weeks before the British surrender at Yorktown.

Another prominent family that settled the Valley was the Bryans of the Great Spring of west Salem. William Bryan Sr., known in family lore as "The Emigrant," was born in Ireland but traveled to the colonies in 1718 to escape religious persecution. Settling first in the vicinity of Salem, New Jersey, he moved with his growing family to the Roanoke Valley about 1746. They made their home on 400 acres between the river and the Great Spring that would someday fill the ponds at Lake Spring Park.

Grave marker for William Bryan Sr., his wife Margaret, and his son William Bryan Jr., placed in the 1920s in West Hill Cemetery by Bryan descendants.

Bryan family tradition records a narrow escape from an early Indian raid on the area. The family fled in canoes down the river and temporarily relocated to Pennsylvania; they returned two years later to find nothing left of their farm but one cat and one rooster. The Bryans rebuilt, and William the Emigrant lived here until his death in 1789, supposedly at the age of 104, although his gravestone lists the death date as 1786. His family is often credited with making an indelible mark on our area: it is thought by many that they brought the name "Salem" with them from their prior home in Salem, New Jersey.

Another interesting early denizen was Frederick "Indian" Garst. The Garst family came to the area in the mid-18th century, and Frederick eventually settled along Green Ridge in an old log home/fort that was demolished to make room for I-581. He later moved to the Mason Creek area, where his descendants would operate a mill, later known as Kesler's Mill. Frederick got his interesting nickname from a legendary account of an Indian attack. One day when Garst was chopping wood, Indians approached clearly intending to kill him. Frederick communicated to them his desire to finish splitting a large log so that his family might have heat for the winter. Obligingly, the Indians gathered on either side of the log and placed their hands in the split to help pull it apart. Frederick then knocked the wedge out of the log, trapping the attackers by the hands, and proceeded to kill them.

The gravestone of Frederick "Indian" Garst.

Center: An 18th Century pistol purported to have belonged to Andrew Lewis.

By the turn of the 19th century, several dozen families had established homesteads scattered about in this corner of what was then Botetourt County. The Great Wagon Road, today's Routes 11 and 460, continually brought new settlers and passersby heading west. In fact, the distinguished personage of Louis Phillippe, the future French king, was one such traveler in 1797—only five years before the town of Salem was formed. His diary describes his passage through the area with few accolades for southwest Virginia. At a tavern in nearby Daleville, he depicts a group heading for Kentucky as rather uncouth, with "some who never shut up for a moment and others who never said a word but could not stop yawning, scratching, belching, etc." On his way through Salem, Louis Phillippe dined at the Coles' estate on the west end of Salem. He was rather unmoved by his visit, finding "(t)he countryside unimpressive except here and there (with g)reenery thick, and in the oak forests whole groves... green."

Despite its lack of amenities to impress French royalty, the Valley was steadily growing, with more adventurers passing by daily and more opportunities for businesses serving travelers. Indeed it was not long before an enterprising settler decided to form a town along this well-trodden pathway. ❦

2

730 for in One Certain Tract or Parcel of Land in
the County aforesaid containing Ninety six Acres & half
of an Acre be the same more or less & lying on the [illegible]
side of Roan oak river being the Land whereon the said
Benjamin Whitenack lately lived which sd Land is bounded
as followeth to wit Begining at a white oak & Pine corner
to said Tract & [illegible] thence S84°E 116 Poles to three
Oak saplins corner to the same S4°E 240 Poles to a large
pine & white oak & Black oak saplings thence a straight
course to the Begining To have & to hold the said Land &
Premises with all & singular its appurtenances unto the
said John H. Maxwell & to his Heirs & assigns for ever &
they the said Benjamin Whitenack & Martha his
wife doth hereby covenant with the said John H.
Maxwell that they will warrant & defend the
said Land & Premises from them & their Heirs &
from the claim or claims of all other men &
manner of Persons whatsoever unto the said John
H. Maxwell & to his Heirs & assigns for ever In Witness whereof the said Benjamin Whitenack & Martha his wife hath hereunto set their Hands
& Seals the day & year first above written

Benjamin Whitenack (Seal)
(Seal)

At Botetourt June Court 1802
This Indenture of Bargain and Sale was acknowledged in Court by the within mentioned
Benjamin Whitenack and ordered to be recorded

A Copy Teste H. Bowyer Clk

731 Simpson to Cole — This Indenture made the 4th day of June
in the Year of our Lord One thousand Eight hundred &
two Between James Simpson & Eleanor his wife of Botetourt County & State of Virginia of the one Part and
Susanna Cole of the County & State aforesaid of the
other Part Witnesseth that for and in consideration of
twenty Dollars in hand paid by the said Susanna
Cole to the said James Simpson the receipt whereof
is hereby acknowledged by the said James Simpson
hath granted bargained sold aliened and confirmed
and by these Presents doth give grant Bargain sell
alien and confirm unto the said Susanna Cole and to
her Heirs & assigns for ever One certain Lott or piece
of Ground situate in the County aforesaid whereon
the said Susanna Cole now liveth which Lott or piece
of Ground is in a plan of a Town laid off by the
said James Simpson near where sd Simpson now
lives which Town is now known by the name of Salem
& which Lott is numbered Nineteen lying on the North
West side of Roan oak Street joining on the East
side of an alley of 16 ft wide and is four poles
in front & sixteen Poles back at right Angles
with the appurtenances thereunto belonging To have
and to hold the said Lott piece or Parcel of Land
hereby granted Bargained and sold with all and
singular the appurtenances thereunto belonging to
her the said Susanna Cole & to her Heirs and
Assigns for ever to the only proper use & behoof
of her the said Susanna Cole and of her Heirs
& assigns forever And the said James Simpson &
Eleanor his wife for themselves their Heirs Execu-
tors and administrators doth hereby Covenant

A Flourishing Place

1802~1852

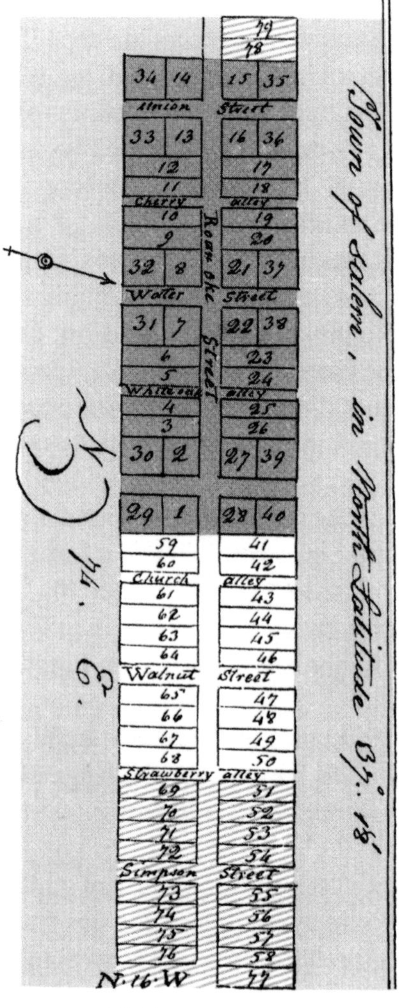

LEGEND
ORIGINAL TOWN OF SALEM - 1806
EXPANSION OF 1813
EXPANSION OF 1829 [1848]
EXPANSION OF 1850

Map showing the new town's early growth from Norwood C. Middleton's Salem: A Virginia Chronicle.

Paul and Nancy Collins (as James Simpson and Susanna Cole) reenact the historic 1802 deed signing for the Salem Museum's Bicentennial Ghost Walk.

Previous page: Salem's "Birth Certificate Deed" between James Simpson and Susanna Cole, Botetourt County Deed Book 7, page 731.

On a late spring day in the first pulse of the 19th century, the town of Salem, Virginia, was born. Her birth certificate? A deed in the Botetourt County courthouse, recording a $20 land transaction between James Simpson and Susanna Cole on June 4, 1802.

James Simpson, founder of the town, remains a bit of an ambiguous character in our local heritage. His birth date and place, parentage, and eventual fate are all lost to the vacuum of history. What is known is that in 1800, he purchased from William Lewis (a son of Andrew) 31 acres of land astride the Great Road. His plans for the land were soon made clear: to lay out a grid of lots and establish a town. Susanna Cole, a wealthy single woman, was the first to take advantage of Simpson's offer and purchased her lot at the northeast corner of modern Main Street and Cherry Alley, in a "town laid off by the said James Simpson...which town is now known by the name of Salem."

Simpson sold 21 other lots in 1802, only two in 1803, but more than a dozen in 1804. In that year, for reasons that will likely never be known, Simpson sold virtually all of his Virginia holdings for $6,666 to Johannes Brugh and left for Alabama, where he apparently died in the 1820s.

Little is remembered about Salem's founding father today, and still less about her founding mother, Susanna Cole. One tradition records that she was the survivor of an Indian abduction, while another more reliable account claims it was her sister. Records indicate that she never married, and that she became rather well-to-do in the new community. Slightly more is known of her brother John Cole, who lived west of town in a "brick mansion" that very likely still stands today as Preston Place.

In 1805, residents of the new town applied to the state legislature to establish Salem officially. This application provides the earliest description of Salem on record: in a "fertile part" of Botetourt County, "proprietors have made good buildings and settled, and sundry others are now building—which from the present appearance must make it in a short time a flourishing place—as it lies on a very eligible spot and in the midst of a wealthy and populous part of the said county—being at the junction of the roads from your seat of government and from the northward leading to the western country and where the farmers and others may find a market for their produce and be conveniently supplied with such materials as they may be in need of as there are a number of mechanics and some vendors of merchandise resident therein."

The oldest surviving building in Salem may be West Main Street's Preston Place, dating perhaps as far back as 1788. On this site John Cole (a brother of Susanna) lived in a "brick mansion" visited by a young Davy Crockett and French Prince Louis Phillippe. The Cole house appears along the Great Wagon Road on the adjoining Botetourt County map, made in 1821 by John Woods.

Even though the earliest settlers' histories are largely obscured by time, we can see the sequel to their stories around us every day. For a number of reasons, Salem did indeed soon become a "flourishing place."

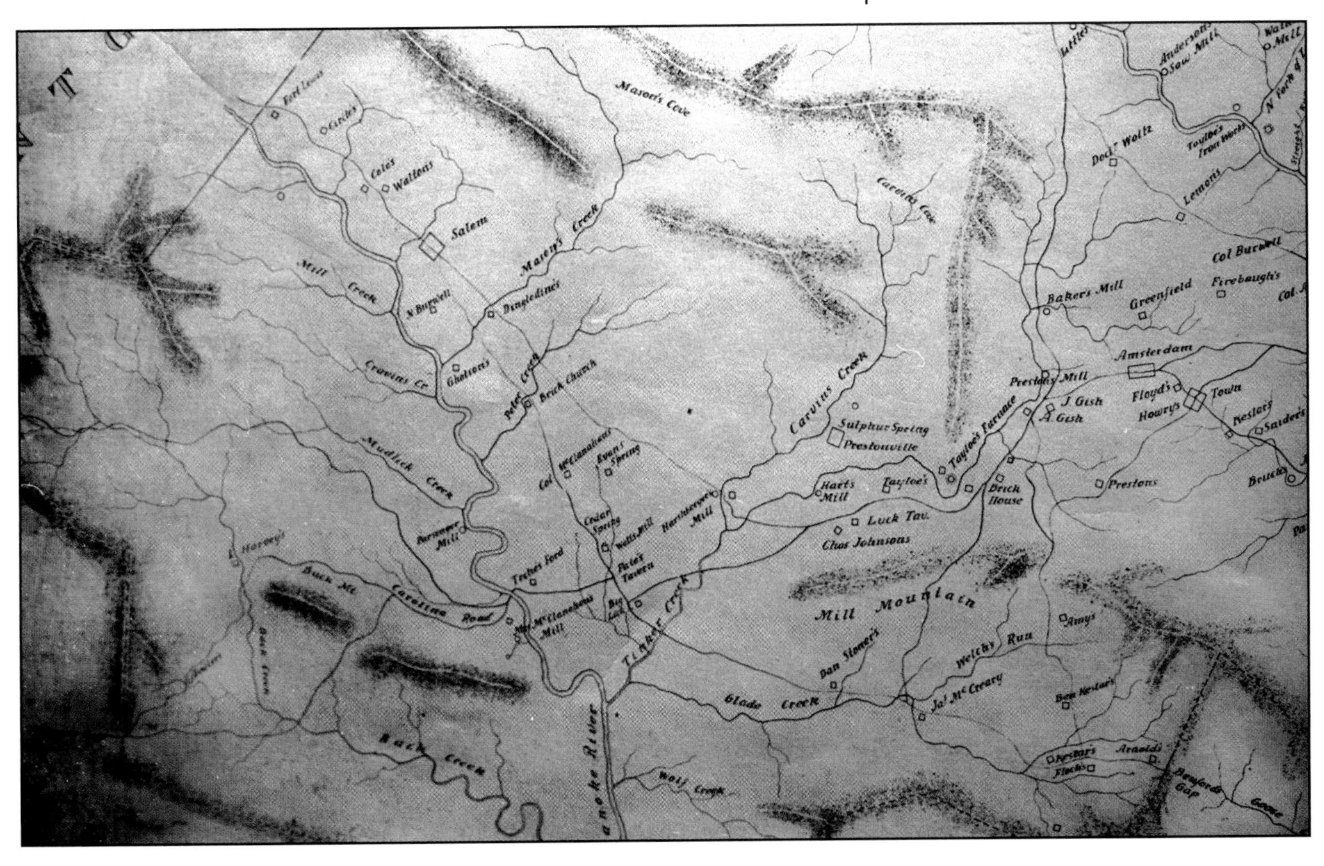

NEW STORE.

The subscriber respectfully announces to the citizens of Salem and its vicinity, that he has opened to-day in Salem, an entirely new stock of Goods recently purchased in the Northern Cities at very reduced prices; consequently it enables him to sell accordingly. His stock consists of

DRY GOODS,

GROCERIES,

HARDWARE, QUEENSWARE,

CLOTHING, SHOES, &c.

Amongst the Dry Goods, are Broad Cloths, Cassimeres, Kentucky Jeans, Satinets, Tweeds, Kerseys, Gloves, and Suspenders.

The Groceries are fresh and a large and general assortment, which I deem unnecessary to enumerate.

I invite the public to call and examine my stock which I now offer very low for cash or country produce.

I hope by being strict and use the best of my exertions to please, to gain a part of public patronage.

E. GERST.

Salem, Va. 1848.

The Great Wagon Road that the new town straddled was among the prime causes of Salem's quick growth. This road, one of the main thoroughfares from Pennsylvania to the western lands of Tennessee and Kentucky, was heavily traveled and thus brought a great deal of business to Salem. For the first generation or so, Salem must have been known primarily as a "tavern town." Such whimsical names as the Globe, the Indian Queen, the Leather Bottle, and the Star and Garter could be seen on colorful signs hanging above Roanoke (today's Main) Street. Perhaps the best known was Griffin Lamkin's Mermaid Tavern, just outside of town about where Chestnut Street intersects Burwell. It featured not only hospitable entertainment, but also a quarter-mile race track. One early visitor of the "Mairmaid" was Andrew Jackson, whose travels through "Salum" on his frequent treks from Tennessee to Washington are recorded in his precariously spelled letters. While there is no explicit record of President James Polk, another Tennesseean, staying in early Salem, his papers record travels along the Great Road, and it is likely he stopped at local inns as well from time to time.

This sketch of the headquarters of the Roanoke Navigation Company was made in 1930, just before the building at Union and Main was torn down.

The Great Road brought more than just taverns to Salem, and the main street was soon teeming with blacksmiths, physicians, general stores, mills, wagon repair shops, and other enterprises intended to serve travelers and townsfolk alike. As is often the case, growth bred growth; within a few years, ancillary roads and turnpikes were being constructed to connect Salem to other areas, especially Lynchburg.

While roadways provided the fundamental transportation system of the early 19th century, dreams of something even greater flowed on the river. An optimistic, but ultimately futile, attempt to link Salem to the sea presents another reason for the town's prosperity.

In 1816, the Roanoke Navigation Company was chartered in an attempt to make the Roanoke River navigable to cargo-bearing boats as far south and east as Weldon, NC. If this venture were successful, trade goods could bypass the virtually impenetrable web of mountain roads, and as one of the Navigation Company's hubs, Salem would become a thriving center of trade. Tradition has it that one of these boats managed to journey along the shallows of the river and arrive in Salem as early as 1818. Within the decade, company records claimed that there was "tolerable good and safe navigation to and from Salem." Still, this ambitious scheme never fully paid off, and it was not long before the whole idea had been made obsolete by better roads and the advent of railroads. Regardless of the ultimate failure of the Roanoke Navigation Company, the idea that Salem could become a

Center: Williams-Brown House (today home of the Salem Museum) was built as a store and a residence about 1845 by William C. Williams.

This handwritten advertisement and one year warranty was pasted inside the top drawer of the 1828 bureau (below) made in Salem by carpenter John Wilbert.

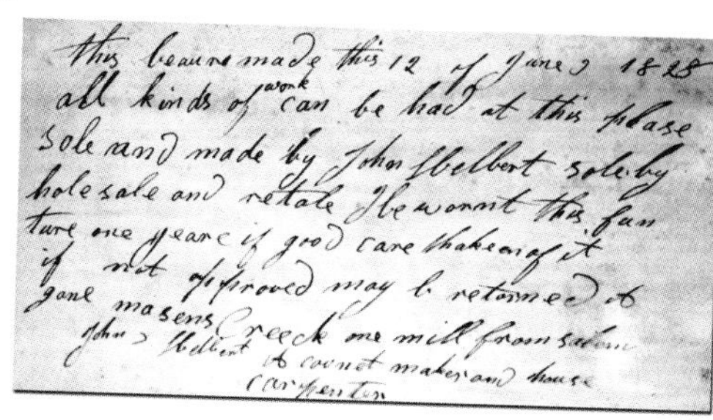

this beaurow made this 12 of janey 1828
all kinds of work can be had at this plase
sole and made by John Wilbert solely
hole sale and retale I he warrant this fun
ture one yeare if good care thaken of it
if not approved may be returned at
jane masens creek one mill from salem
John Wilbert a coanet maker and house
carpenter

Spoons made ca. 1850 by Salem silversmith John Withers.

Handmade Valentine from 1830 that has been passed down for generations in the McCauley family. Perhaps it was originally sent by John McCauley to his first wife, Cynthia.

economic center spawned a wave of building and development from the teens to the thirties.

Another important impetus for Salem's growth came in 1838, when Roanoke County was carved out of Botetourt County at the behest of local legislator John McCauley. Salem, as the only community of any size near the nucleus of the newly formed region, was chosen as the county seat. With that distinction came a courthouse, government offices and frequent visitors from throughout the valley. Anyone getting a marriage license, recording a deed or will, paying taxes, or appearing in a court case was obliged to come to Salem—and while here, why not shop in one of the numerous stores, eat or stay overnight in a tavern, or trade a horse in "Jockey Alley," all business that previously would have gone to Fincastle. As county seat, Salem was destined to become for a time the leading community of the Roanoke Valley.

John McCauley, the "founder" of Roanoke County. His lobbying efforts in Richmond were instrumental in the Roanoke Valley's split from Botetourt County.

Within a few years, Salem was transformed from a tavern town to a college town by the arrival of Virginia Collegiate Institute from Augusta County. In 1847, Lutheran pastors Dr. David Bittle and Christopher Baughman moved their fledgling school to its new home in Salem, chosen in part due to an active Lutheran population in the Valley. A few years later in 1853, the institute was chartered as a full-fledged college under the name Roanoke. While only a handful of students attended the school's first session in Salem, enrollment rapidly expanded and the college was on firm enough footing that it was one of the few institutions in the South to remain open during the Civil War. From its beginnings, Roanoke College not only offered educational opportunities for Salem sons, but it also attracted students from other

The original Roanoke County courthouse built in 1841 by William C. Williams.

Early view of Roanoke College by Professor Henry Osborne.

George Shanks, Salem's first "Chairman of the Board of Trustees"—in effect the town's first mayor; and below a dress believed to be worn by Shanks' wife, Lucy Lewis.

areas to come spend their time—and dollars—in the growing town.

A final and lasting reason for Salem's expansion fundamentally changed the town, even as it altered the nature of transportation and commerce throughout the United States. In 1852, a half century after Salem's founding, the *John R. McDaniel*, a wood-burning locomotive, chugged into town. The arrival of the Virginia and Tennessee Railroad achieved the goal that the Roanoke Navigation Company never could: linking Salem to the rest of the world through affordable and efficient transportation.

David Bittle, founder of Roanoke College.

Alexander White, owner of west Salem's Fort Lewis mansion. Note the similarities to the Shanks portrait opposite.

To celebrate the railroad's arrival, Salem ended her first half century with a grand party, barbecue, and fireworks display. Residents almost certainly felt a twinge of pride that Simpson's modest village had grown into an energetic little town with an expanding economy, a growing college, and an active courthouse—all linked to the rest of the world by road, rail, and (briefly) water.

Vanished Salem 1

Lake Spring

Clementine and F. J. Chapman soon after their marriage.

Previous page: Detail of Lake Spring Hotel from a period promotional poster.

Souvenir items from Lake Spring.

The imposing hotel overlooking west Main Street.

Imagine Salem as one of the top vacation resorts on the East Coast.

Hard to picture? In fact, for a few shining years Salem was just that: a mountain vacation spot with a national reputation for healthy climate and elegant social charm. At the center of it all was Lake Spring Hotel west of town.

Lake Spring Hotel was opened in 1872 by Flavius Josephus Chapman, a Salem entrepreneur and jack-of-all-trades. Chapman took the resort's name from the spring-fed lakes he dug on the site of William Bryan's old plantation. The lakes served a double purpose: to give recreation to his guests and to act as Salem's new water supply. During the sixteen years Lake Spring existed, it attracted and delighted visitors from around the nation.

Chapman offered a variety of leisure activities catering to refined society: boating, billiards, bowling, baseball, croquet, hunting and fishing expeditions, and night after night of dances.

Not all left happily, however. The story is told of Mary Vose, a tourist from New Orleans who stopped at Lake Spring with her husband. One night they

One of the "rustic cabins" available to guests.

Roanoke Red Sulphur Springs, F. J. Chapman's other resort across Catawba Mountain.

The Chapmans and their guests enjoy the lakes.

strolled up to the nearby West Hill Cemetery (later known as Tank Hill) to enjoy the picturesque view. Mrs. Vose commented on the beauty of the site and said that she would like to be buried in the cemetery. She died that very night, and her last request was granted.

But as a rule, a stay at Lake Spring was considered quite healthy. Visitors were encouraged to extend their stay by taking a stage coach over Catawba Mountain to another resort owned by Mr. Chapman: Roanoke Red Sulphur Springs. Chapman made much of testimonials from guests that the mineral waters at Catawba would cure virtually any disease.

The storybook history of Lake Spring came to an unfortunate end in 1892 when a fire broke out during an elegant dance. Guests turned out in their tuxedos to form a bucket brigade from the lakes to the burning building, but to no avail. The hotel was damaged beyond repair and soon closed. Chapman never recovered from the financial blow and died within two years at the Hotel Lucerne, the last of his three hostelries.

Since the lakes continued to serve the community as a water supply, the town acquired the property

Flavius Josephus Chapman, his wife Clementine, and their children near the ponds.

Guests enjoy the gazebo that stood in the center of the lake.

Lake Spring in its second incarnation: a public park, early in the century and today.

in 1900 and converted it into Salem's first public park. One of the improvements added grace and culture to many a summer afternoon: the gazebo bandstand from the old county courthouse was moved to Lake Spring in 1909. Reminiscent of a bandstand that sat in the center of the lakes during the hotel's hey-day, the new gazebo provided a venue for local musicians to perform and young couples to steal a first kiss.

Within a few years, the streetcar line had been extended to Lake Spring, and flocks of summertime visitors from Roanoke and Vinton made the trek to West Salem to enjoy a picturesque afternoon. When the town briefly closed the park to safeguard the water supply from contamination, howls of protest resulted, and the park was reopened to the delight of all.

More than a century later, the property continues to enchant residents and visitors alike. One of the valley's most beautiful public parks, Lake Spring still bears the storied name of Salem's lost resort. ❦

3

Everything the Heart of Man Could Desire

1852-1902

Chapter 3

Previous page: Detail of Edward's Beyer's View of Salem, *showing the Williams-Brown House on the Great Wagon Road.*

Churches, Blacksmith Shop, and College: A View of Salem, Virginia
by Edward Beyer

Chapter 3

Itinerant German landscape artist Edward Beyer traveled through Virginia in the mid-1850s, painting and sketching towns, homes, resorts, and scenery along the way. In 1855, he visited Salem and was commissioned by Henry Chapman to paint A View of Salem, *a lush panorama of the town's main streets as seen from East Hill. In addition, Beyer captured Bellevue, the home of Dr. Andrew Lewis in the vicinity of today's Mill Lane, and Edgehill (now called Mount Airy), a house still standing on the grounds of the Veterans Administration Hospital.*

Bellevue, the Lewis Homestead
by Edward Beyer

Chapter 3

Edgehill
by Edward Beyer

Chapter 3

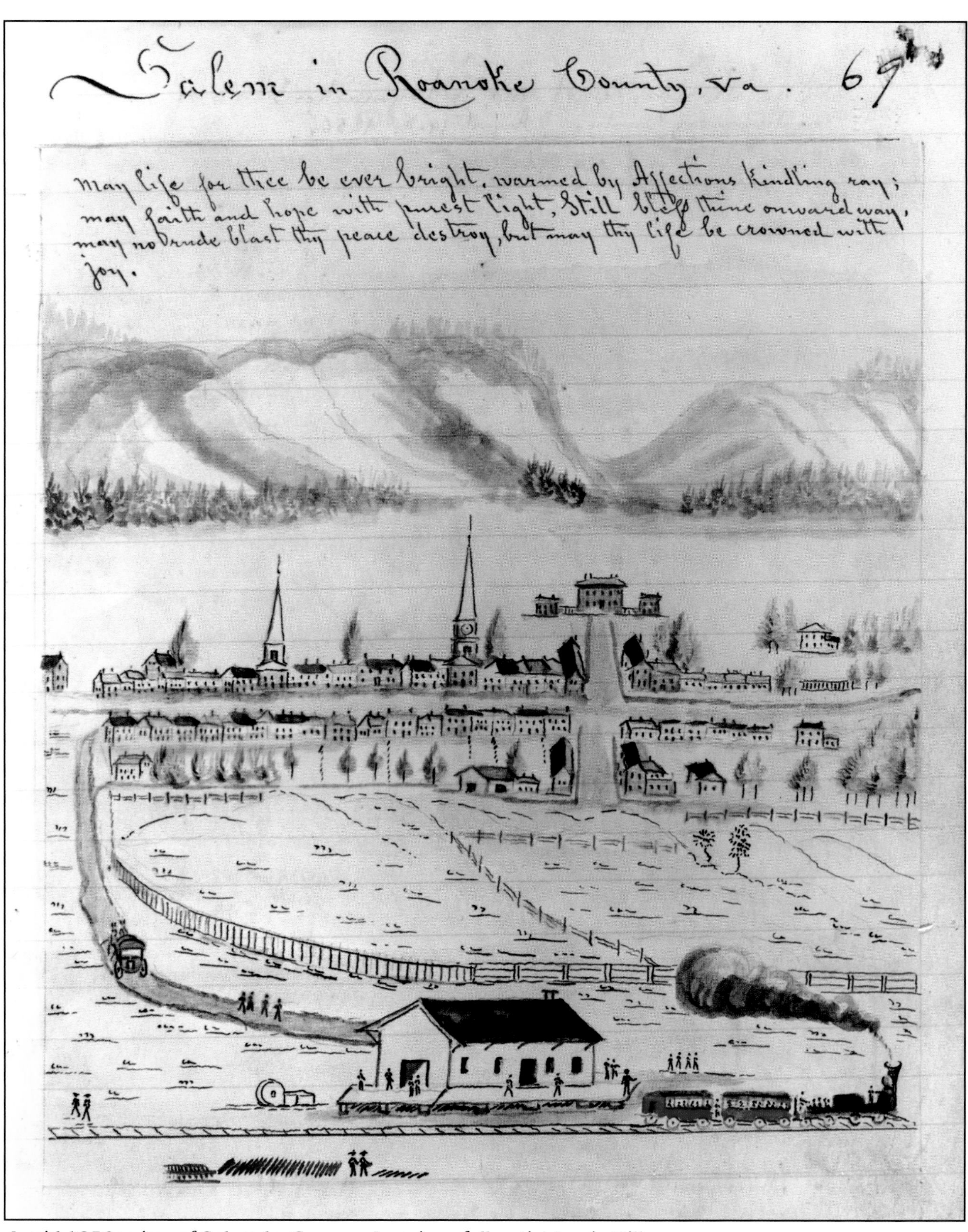

A mid-1850s view of Salem by German-American folk artist Lewis Miller.

Salem's turbulent second half-century would witness war and reconstruction, boom and bust, amazing technological advances, and ultimately the triumph of the Salem spirit.

When German itinerant artist Edward Beyer passed through Salem in 1855, he recorded on canvas a bustling hamlet, still a linear town astride a dirt wagon road, with inns, shops, churches, prominent homes, a courthouse and a college. And further, on opposite outskirts of town, the poetically named estates of Bellevue and Edgehill reveal the grand, orderly plantations of the "gentleman farmer," complete with outbuildings, landscaped yards, and—showing the less than idyllic lives of a considerable population of Salemites—slaves toiling in the fields. In each of Beyer's three paintings of Salem, passersby go about their daily chores as a tiny train chugs through the landscape, drawing the town and its environs into a new era.

While the nation struggled with issues of sectional conflict, tariffs, and slavery, there is scant evidence of what Salemites thought of these great debates. Surviving writings indicate that some openly defended the institution of slavery. David Carter, the editor of the *Salem Weekly Register*, visited New York in 1855 and addressed the issue with a good deal of smug southern paternalism:

> *What southern man, after witnessing the degradation and wretchedness of the poorer classes of a northern city, does not turn with pride to his own country, whose situation are (sic) infinitely preferable? Who would not rather be in a state of bondage on a southern plantation, than be a servile menial in the North, where toiling thousands barely earn a support?*

Carter, of course, could not speak for the approximately one-third of the county's population that was African-American. His view was likely that of many whites, only a small portion of whom owned slaves. For the most part, southern sentiment among landowners ran high in the Roanoke Valley, as evidenced by the fact that Lincoln received not a single vote from the county in 1860.

When the Civil War erupted in 1861, Salem found herself on the edges of the storm. The war would in-

Folk artist Lewis Miller.

A view of Salem at a
the river roanoke, and

in Roanoke County,
of hills. near the Blue ridge

Lewis Miller's sketch of town as seen from the Fort Lewis area.

Salem's bylaws severely restricted the movement of slaves and free blacks in 1859, just before the Civil War broke out.

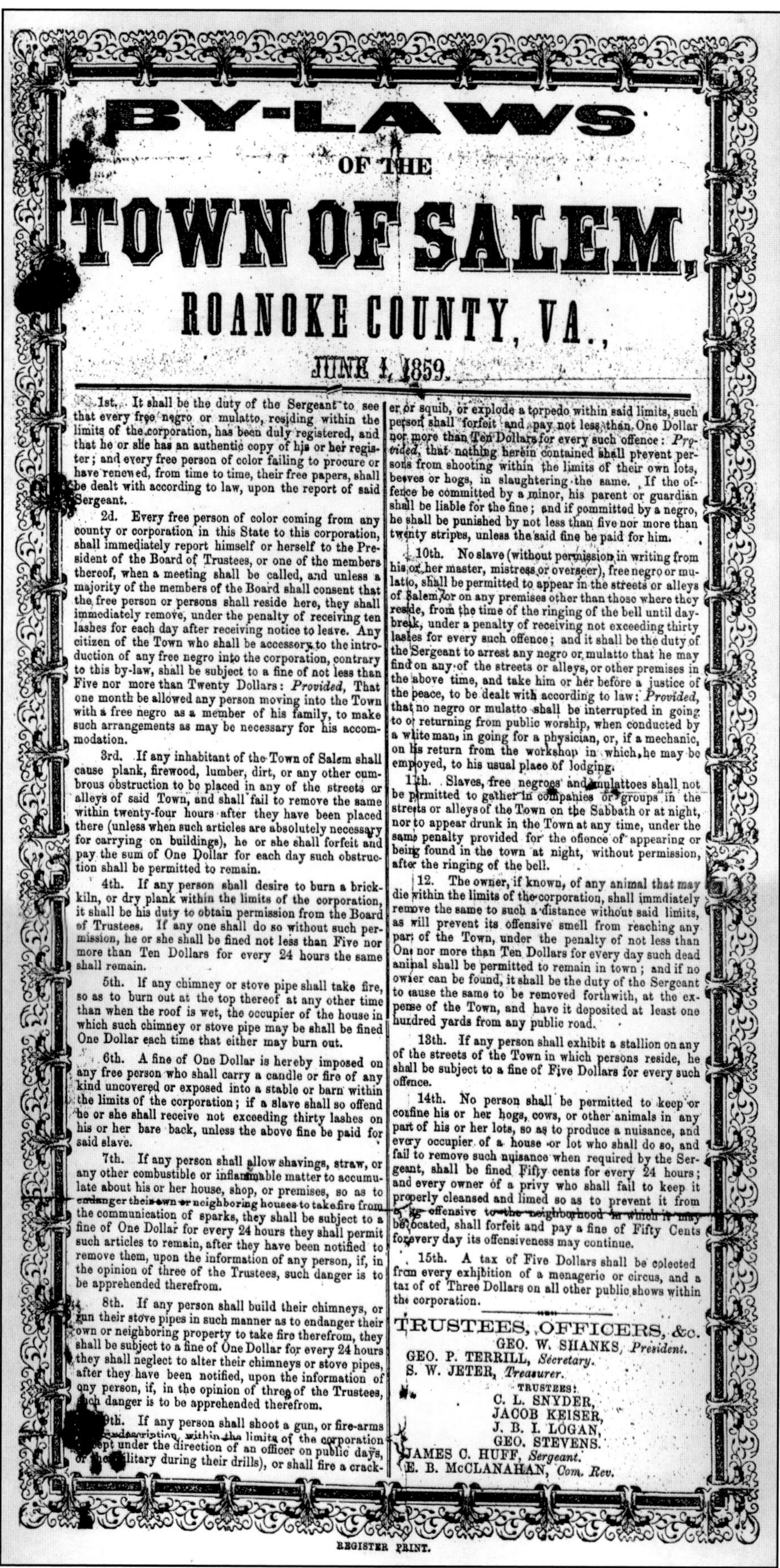

BY-LAWS

OF THE

TOWN OF SALEM,

ROANOKE COUNTY, VA.,

JUNE 1, 1859.

1st. It shall be the duty of the Sergeant to see that every free negro or mulatto, residing within the limits of the corporation, has been duly registered, and that he or she has an authentic copy of his or her register; and every free person of color failing to procure or have renewed, from time to time, their free papers, shall be dealt with according to law, upon the report of said Sergeant.

2d. Every free person of color coming from any county or corporation in this State to this corporation, shall immediately report himself or herself to the President of the Board of Trustees, or one of the members thereof, when a meeting shall be called, and unless a majority of the members of the Board shall consent that the free person or persons shall reside here, they shall immediately remove, under the penalty of receiving ten lashes for each day after receiving notice to leave. Any citizen of the Town who shall be accessory to the introduction of any free negro into the corporation, contrary to this by-law, shall be subject to a fine of not less than Five nor more than Twenty Dollars: *Provided*, That one month be allowed any person moving into the Town with a free negro as a member of his family, to make such arrangements as may be necessary for his accommodation.

3rd. If any inhabitant of the Town of Salem shall cause plank, firewood, lumber, dirt, or any other cumbrous obstruction to be placed in any of the streets or alleys of said Town, and shall fail to remove the same within twenty-four hours after they have been placed there (unless when such articles are absolutely necessary for carrying on buildings), he or she shall forfeit and pay the sum of One Dollar for each day such obstruction shall be permitted to remain.

4th. If any person shall desire to burn a brick-kiln, or dry plank within the limits of the corporation, it shall be his duty to obtain permission from the Board of Trustees. If any one shall do so without such permission, he or she shall be fined not less than Five nor more than Ten Dollars for every 24 hours the same shall remain.

5th. If any chimney or stove pipe shall take fire, so as to burn out at the top thereof at any other time than when the roof is wet, the occupier of the house in which such chimney or stove pipe may be shall be fined One Dollar each time that either may burn out.

6th. A fine of One Dollar is hereby imposed on any free person who shall carry a candle or fire of any kind uncovered or exposed into a stable or barn within the limits of the corporation; if a slave shall so offend he or she shall receive not exceeding thirty lashes on his or her bare back, unless the above fine be paid for said slave.

7th. If any person shall allow shavings, straw, or any other combustible or inflammable matter to accumulate about his or her house, shop, or premises, so as to endanger their own or neighboring houses to take fire from the communication of sparks, they shall be subject to a fine of One Dollar for every 24 hours they shall permit such articles to remain, after they have been notified to remove them, upon the information of any person, if, in the opinion of three of the Trustees, such danger is to be apprehended therefrom.

8th. If any person shall build their chimneys, or run their stove pipes in such manner as to endanger their own or neighboring property to take fire therefrom, they shall be subject to a fine of One Dollar for every 24 hours they shall neglect to alter their chimneys or stove pipes, after they have been notified, upon the information of any person, if, in the opinion of three of the Trustees, such danger is to be apprehended therefrom.

9th. If any person shall shoot a gun, or fire-arms of any description, within the limits of the corporation (except under the direction of an officer on public days, or the military during their drills), or shall fire a cracker or squib, or explode a torpedo within said limits, such person shall forfeit and pay not less than One Dollar nor more than Ten Dollars for every such offence: *Provided*, that nothing herein contained shall prevent persons from shooting within the limits of their own lots, beeves or hogs, in slaughtering the same. If the offence be committed by a minor, his parent or guardian shall be liable for the fine; and if committed by a negro, he shall be punished by not less than five nor more than twenty stripes, unless the said fine be paid for him.

10th. No slave (without permission in writing from his or her master, mistress or overseer), free negro or mulatto, shall be permitted to appear in the streets or alleys of Salem, or on any premises other than those where they reside, from the time of the ringing of the bell until daybreak, under a penalty of receiving not exceeding thirty lashes for every such offence; and it shall be the duty of the Sergeant to arrest any negro or mulatto that he may find on any of the streets or alleys, or other premises in the above time, and take him or her before a justice of the peace, to be dealt with according to law: *Provided*, that no negro or mulatto shall be interrupted in going to or returning from public worship, when conducted by a white man, in going for a physician, or, if a mechanic, on his return from the workshop in which he may be employed, to his usual place of lodging.

11th. Slaves, free negroes and mulattoes shall not be permitted to gather in companies or groups in the streets or alleys of the Town on the Sabbath or at night, nor to appear drunk in the Town at any time, under the same penalty provided for the offence of appearing or being found in the town at night, without permission, after the ringing of the bell.

12. The owner, if known, of any animal that may die within the limits of the corporation, shall immdiately remove the same to such a distance without said limits, as will prevent its offensive smell from reaching any part of the Town, under the penalty of not less than One nor more than Ten Dollars for every day such dead animal shall be permitted to remain in town; and if no owner can be found, it shall be the duty of the Sergeant to cause the same to be removed forthwith, at the expense of the Town, and have it deposited at least one hundred yards from any public road.

13th. If any person shall exhibit a stallion on any of the streets of the Town in which persons reside, he shall be subject to a fine of Five Dollars for every such offence.

14th. No person shall be permitted to keep or confine his or her hogs, cows, or other animals in any part of his or her lots, so as to produce a nuisance, and every occupier of a house or lot who shall do so, and fail to remove such nuisance when required by the Sergeant, shall be fined Fifty cents for every 24 hours; and every owner of a privy who shall fail to keep it properly cleansed and limed so as to prevent it from being offensive to the neighborhood in which it may be located, shall forfeit and pay a fine of Fifty Cents for every day its offensiveness may continue.

15th. A tax of Five Dollars shall be colected from every exhibition of a menagerie or circus, and a tax of of Three Dollars on all other public shows within the corporation.

TRUSTEES, OFFICERS, &c.

GEO. W. SHANKS, *President.*
GEO. P. TERRILL, *Secretary.*
S. W. JETER, *Treasurer.*

TRUSTEES:

C. L. SNYDER,
JACOB KEISER,
J. B. I. LOGAN,
GEO. STEVENS.

JAMES C. HUFF, *Sergeant.*
E. B. McCLANAHAN, *Com. Rev.*

REGISTER PRINT.

Civil War cannon ball found underground in the 1990s when brick sidewalks in front of Snyder's Nursing Home on Main Street were replaced.

trude into the valley only twice: once in December 1863 when Union General William Averell raided the town to cut the crucial railroad supplying the Confederate front lines, and again in June 1864 when Confederate General John McCausland fought a small pitched conflict with David Hunter's forces at Hanging Rock. Thus, Salem avoided much of the disastrous calamity that afflicted other southern towns.

That is not to say that Salem families went untouched by the war. Our area sent four units into the fray, and Salem men fought in virtually all of the war's major battles, from Manassas through Gettysburg right up to Appomattox. Two families in particular, the Deyerles and the Griffins, saw more than a fair share of the war.

To speak of military history in Salem is to speak of the Deyerle family. Three of the four Roanoke County units serving the Confederacy were commanded by Deyerles. Madison Pitzer Deyerle formed the Roanoke Grays, attached to the 28th Virginia Infantry under Gen-

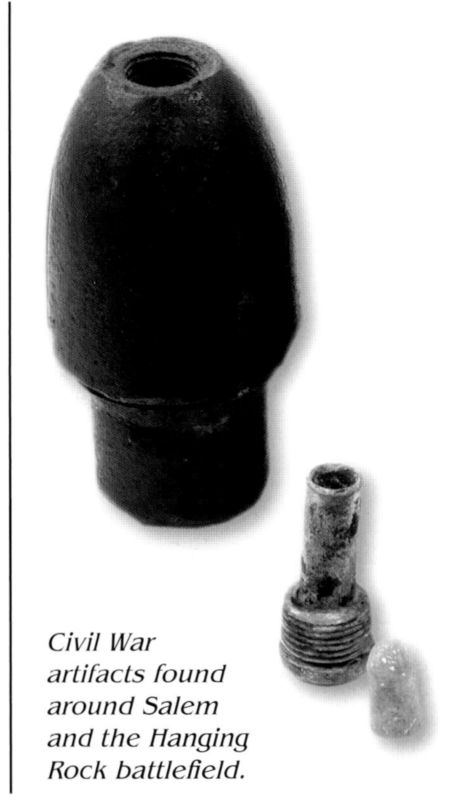

Civil War artifacts found around Salem and the Hanging Rock battlefield.

Collage of unidentified local Confederate soldiers, assembled for Roanoke County's centennial celebration in 1938 and hung in the courthouse.

This 1990s watercolor by Ellen Morris shows an ariel view of the Battle of Hanging Rock, the only engagement in the Roanoke Valley, June 21, 1864.

The Deyerles: brothers Madison Pitzer, John Scott, Ballard Preston, Charles Peter, and cousin Andrew Jackson.

eral Lee. His brother John Scott Deyerle founded the Roanoke Guards, which was mustered into the 54th Virginia and fought primarily in the western theater of the war. Ballard Preston Deyerle, although only sixteen years old, served first under brother John and later in a cavalry unit. Finally, cousin Andrew Jackson Deyerle organized the Dixie Grays as part of the 42nd Virginia Infantry, acted as a military recruiter, and served near the end of the war in the Virginia legislature.

In an interesting aside, one Deyerle brother, Charles Peter, never lived to wear the gray. Charles served in the Mexican War as a surgeon; afterwards he was stationed in California where he died in 1853. His remains were transported back to Salem in an epic post-mortem journey across the isthmus of Panama.

Of the Deyerle family, a local newspaper wrote, "Many homes in the Southland furnished their quota of gallant, courageous and heroic soldier boys, but it would be difficult to find in the broad confines of this Union a home that furnished more distinguished, brave, heroic soldiers than did the (house of) Deyerle."

The "Fighting Griffins" certainly did their part as well. Charles Beale Griffin served in the Salem Flying Artillery and rose to command the unit after the death of founder Abraham Hupp. At Appomattox Court House, the Flying Artillery claimed the honor of firing the last artillery shot of Lee's Army of Northern

William Edward Brown (center) was a private in the Salem Flying Artillery and a resident of the Williams-Brown House. In a letter home to his parents Joshua and Mary (left and right) in September, 1863, he wrote: "I believe with General Lee that unless we capture a Corps of the enemy's it will have but little effect in shortening the war. I am in hopes we will have a battle with Meade in a few days and whip him handsomely. I am in for anything to stop the war with all the rights of the South on a sound footing." This letter was somehow sealed in a wall at the Brown House and found only in the 1990s during renovations to convert the home to a museum.

This 1896 portrait shows William Edward Brown in the comfort of his living room thirty years after the Civil War. He and his wife Carrie Pillow Brown are seated on either side of five of their six daughters. Perched in front are Annie and Carrie, in the middle chair is Mary, and standing in back are Eloise and Bessie.

Abraham Hupp (above), tinsmith and founder of the Salem Flying Artillery; and the soldiers Charles, John, Samuel, and Wingfield Griffin (shown here in his Spanish American War uniform).

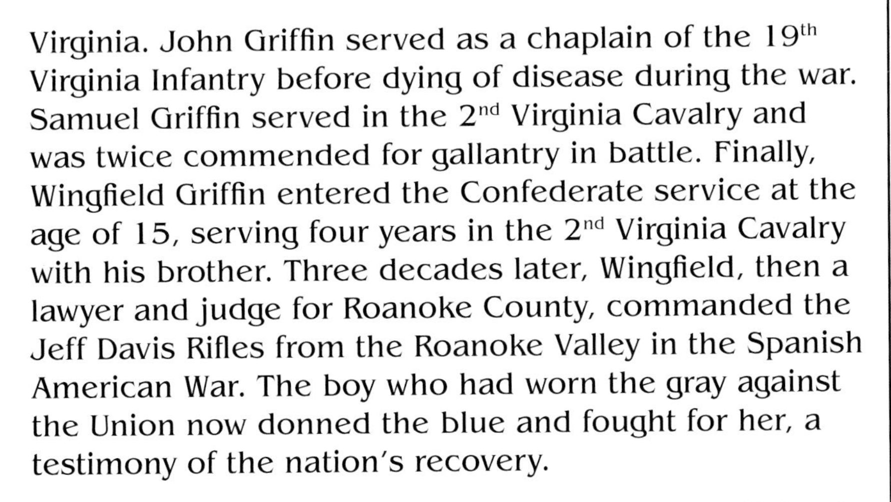

Virginia. John Griffin served as a chaplain of the 19th Virginia Infantry before dying of disease during the war. Samuel Griffin served in the 2nd Virginia Cavalry and was twice commended for gallantry in battle. Finally, Wingfield Griffin entered the Confederate service at the age of 15, serving four years in the 2nd Virginia Cavalry with his brother. Three decades later, Wingfield, then a lawyer and judge for Roanoke County, commanded the Jeff Davis Rifles from the Roanoke Valley in the Spanish American War. The boy who had worn the gray against the Union now donned the blue and fought for her, a testimony of the nation's recovery.

When the War Between the States was over, Salem's boys in gray returned home to a different world, one of hardship and deprivation. Not until the 1870s did the town resume her growth and prosperity. More businesses, homes and churches were constructed. Public schools first appeared in 1872. And Salem acquired a reputation as a resort town, drawing eager visitors from across the nation to the healthy climate of the mountains.

Meanwhile, a separate history was unfolding south of Main Street. Soon after Emancipation, several former slaves of Nathaniel Burwell, one of the county's largest slaveholders, bought lots along newly laid-out streets of

Freed slaves of Nathaniel Burwell's Dropmore Plantation remained close long after Emancipation, and even returned for reunions in 1903 (above) and 1910 (right). The Logan family, descendants of Burwell, hosted the gatherings at the estate, then called Sherwood.

the growing town. Their purchases marked the birth of a separate community, identified by race, along a thoroughfare known as Water Street (today's South Broad). Water Street and adjacent blocks soon encompassed Salem's leading African-American community, where the primary businesses, churches, social organizations and the public school would be located for generations. It was a close-knit, supportive, and prosperous community, but one excluded from the larger Salem society by the racial conventions of the day.

The 1880s found Salem in the midst of a fierce competition over the dominant business of the day: railroads. The newly formed Norfolk and Western Railroad announced that it would build a new connection somewhere in the Roanoke Valley, complete with railroad shops and a hotel. Salem, as the county seat and largest community in the area, felt certain that she would be chosen. This confidence was misguided, however, and the neighboring village of Big Lick convinced the N&W to build there instead. Soon, Big Lick became the thriving railroad city of Roanoke, and Salem was left bewildered.

Salem's African American school on Water Street, known successively as Graded School A and the Roanoke County Training School.

Principal John Duckwilder and the faculty of the school.

An unidentified member of the prominent Duckwilder family.

This photograph by the local Maury Brothers studio is believed to be John Duckwilder.

Unidentified man with possums outside of College Lutheran Church at the corner of College and Main.

This somewhat idealized view of town from an 1891 promotional pamphlet shows a bustling valley at the foot of Twelve O'clock Knob.

Salem Railroad Depot, built 1891.

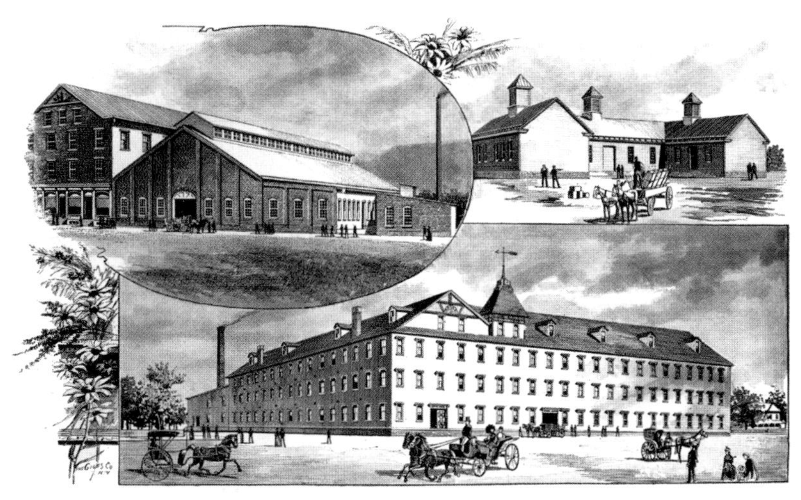

Top: *Promotional sketches of Salem's new businesses. Shown here are the Holstein Woolen Mills, the Chadwick Two-Wheeler Works, and the Salem Gas Heater Factory.*

Bottom: The new iron bridge over the Roanoke River with Salem Rolling Mills inset.

In point of fact, the ensuing years would show that Salem benefited greatly from Roanoke's growth. The late 1880s and early 90s comprise Salem's "Boom Years," when the town expanded enormously. New neighborhoods were opened, new businesses flourished, banks were chartered, and citizens were graced with electric lights, an updated water works, and modern sewer system. In an unprecedented surge, the population doubled between 1880 and 1900, to over 3400 souls.

Primarily responsible for this growth were investment land companies, which sold stock by the handful and purchased the rolling farmland around town for development. Groups such as the Salem Improvement Company, the Salem Development Company and the South Salem Land Company offered enticements to businesses and factories to relocate here, and eagerly sold residential lots to the workers who followed. Descriptions of Salem in the promotional pamphlets of the day were gems of salesmanship—boasting of an idyll "clothed in the garb of beauty and plenteousness" and graced with "well nigh everything that the heart of man could desire." A news writer from Massachusetts touring the South was so impressed (or perhaps pressed upon) by local representatives that he dubbed Salem "the most enthusiastic town in Virginia." And the *Richmond Times Dispatch* boasted that "if the future of Salem as a great industrial center is not assured, then hundreds of men of sagacity and capital are blind."

The sagacious and rich developers were not blind, but perhaps a bit over-optimistic. The boom eventually fizzled out, a victim of nationwide economic downturns and an odd series of natural disasters (including a flood, tornado, and three-foot snow) that ruined homes,

Two leaders of the land boom: W. W. Ballard and J. E. Allemong (boy with bicycle unidentified).

The majestic Hotel Salem on College. This building later served as the Lutheran Orphanage, but was razed in the 1930s to make room for Andrew Lewis High School.

a bridge, and key industrial buildings. Salem's growth spurt, however short lived, did accomplish a fundamental transformation of the town. While Salem never became the "Queen City" of southwest Virginia, as some promotional material predicted, she was able to retain the charm of a small community that knows how to dream big.

Salem closed out her first century with a mammoth Centennial Celebration in June of 1902. The town marked the momentous occasion with a gala parade, the publication of William McCauley's epic *History of Roanoke County*, and a fairyland spectacle entitled *Enchantment*, with a cast of 500. Major Samuel Griffin

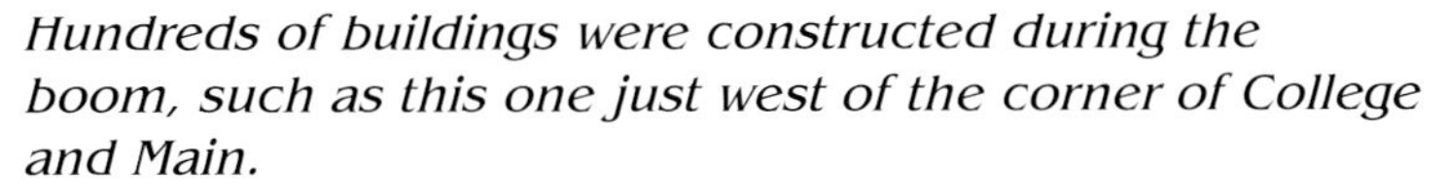

Hundreds of buildings were constructed during the boom, such as this one just west of the corner of College and Main.

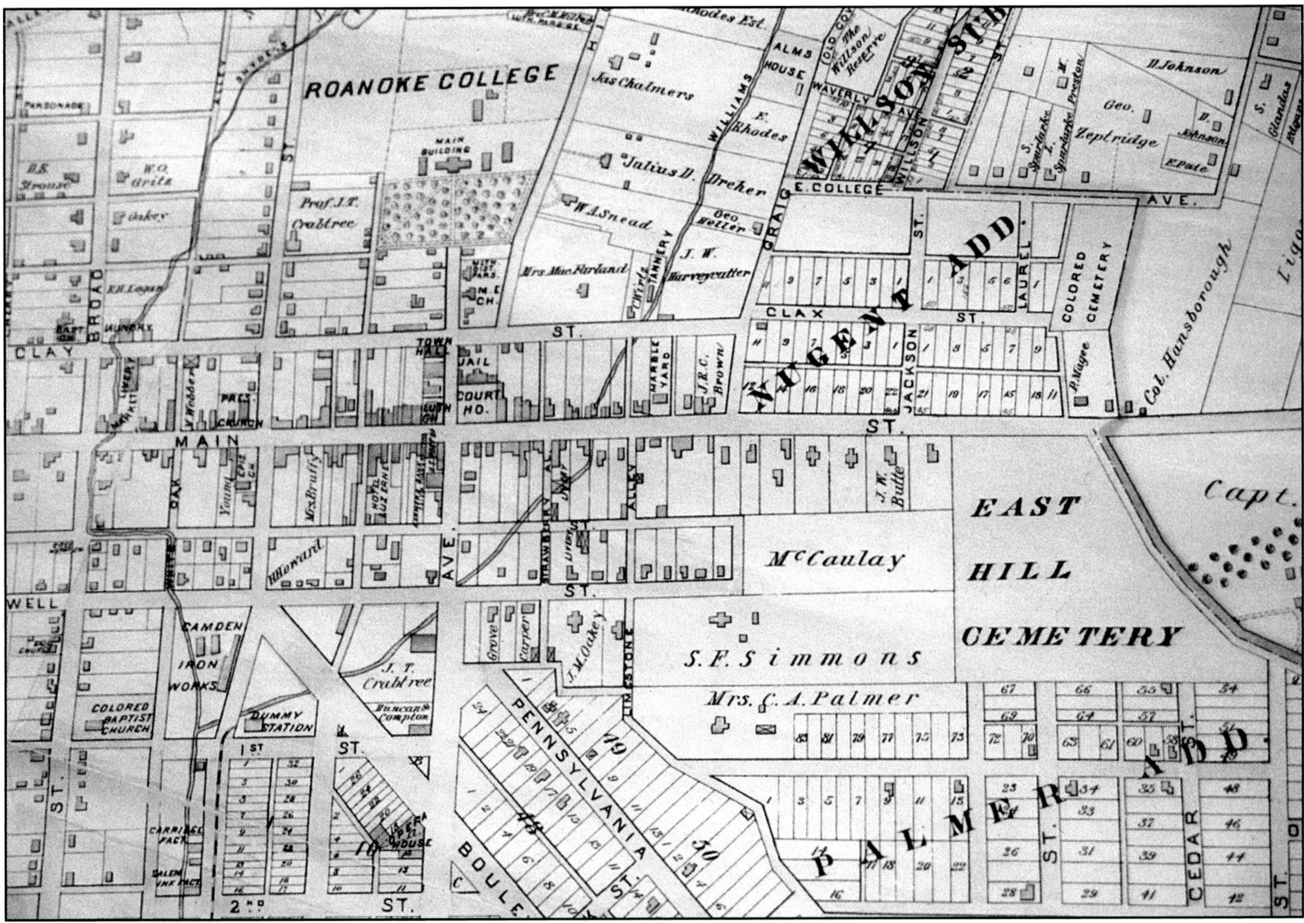

This 1891 Map by the Baist Company includes planned developments as well as existing features. For instance, notice that today's Longwood Park is the residential Nugent Addition.

William McCauley, a leader in planning the Centennial Celebration in 1902. To commemorate the birthday, he authored the epic seven and a half pound tome History of Roanoke County, Salem, Roanoke City, Virginia, and Representative Citizens.

Bunting that wrapped the Centennial floats.

A float of Salem beauties in the Centennial Parade, June 4, 1902.

spoke during the festivities, offering these rousing hopes for Salem's next century:

> *Behind us are a hundred years full of the vicissitudes common to humanity. Love of home and country, joy and sorrow, hope and fear.... These have helped to make our people what they are and our town what it is today.... What will they do for Salem and its people in this second century? Judging by the past we indulge the hope that they will work together for the highest intellectual and moral good of this favored community, and help to fulfill in good measure the present promise of a larger material growth and development. Long live Salem, fair "City of Peace!" May she go on and grow on forever!* ❦

The bustling street of the Centennial Celebration in front of the old Lutheran Church.

Town Sergeant Jacob Frier (right) and Deputy Walter Boone outside of the Town Sergeant's office.

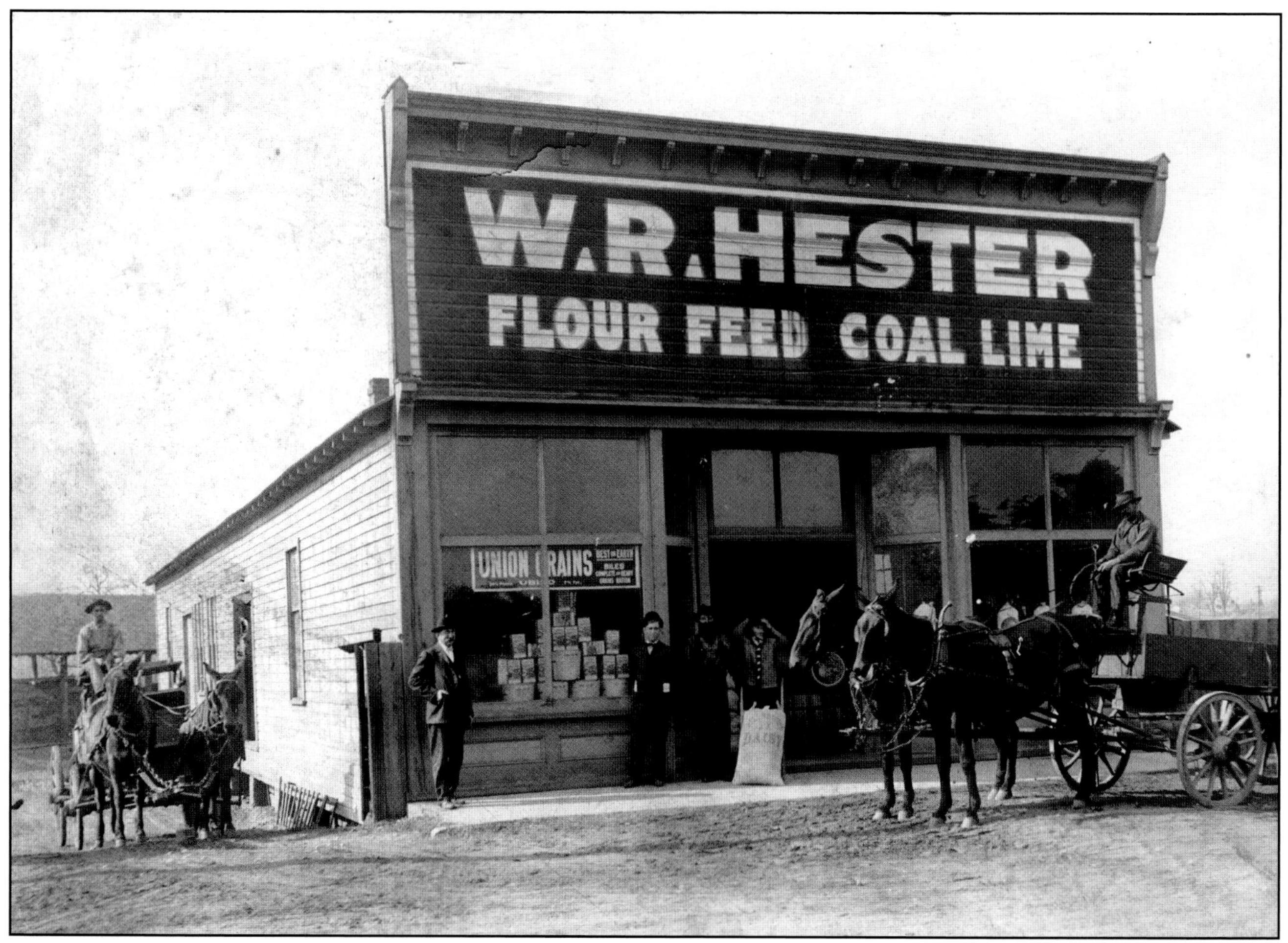

W. R. Hester store on Union Street.

Two Salem business establishments of the era: Shupe Grocery and Finke & McClaugherty Tobacconists.

Salem's favorite gathering place for many years was Dillard's Drugstore. Opening in 1886 as Dillard & Persinger, the pharmacy and soda fountain was on the most prominent corner in town—College and Main.

DILLARD & PERSINGER,
DRUGGISTS
Cor. Main St. & College Ave.
Bell Phone No. 3

Salem, Va. Aug 12th 1907

My dearest little Roby,

I have attempted writing to you twice today at home but Mama & Sister were so bent on talking that I had to repair to the Corner Drug Store and put upon paper some of the things I wish to say to you.

Tomorrow night Tom and I are going over to Roanoke Red to attend a german, my partner's name I do not know, but I have the assurance of a young

Druggists Ed Koontz, Clay Chapman, Blair Dillard, an unidentified man, and Custis Burmell pose outside of Dillard's.

Two photos of the Salem Times-Register *offices on College Avenue. The paper traced its origins to 1854 and, with the exception of the later Civil War years, has been publishing a weekly paper under various names ever since.*

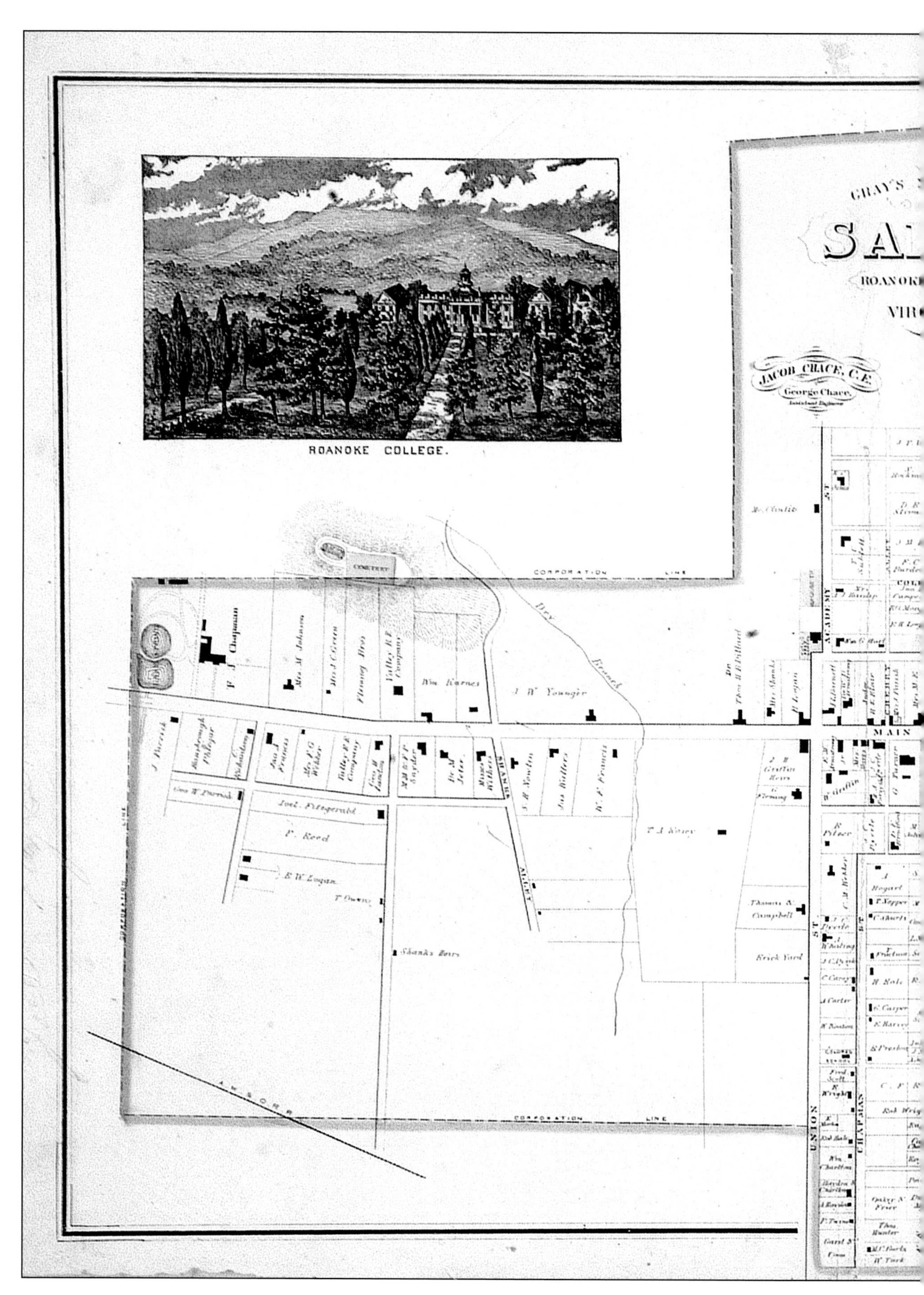
ROANOKE COLLEGE.
JACOB CHACE, C.E.
George Chace,
CORPORATION LINE
CORPORATION LINE
MAIN
ACADEMY ST
UNION
CHAPMAN
CHERRY
J. W. Younger
P. Reed
E. W. Logan
Shanks Heirs
Brick Yard
Thomas & Campbell

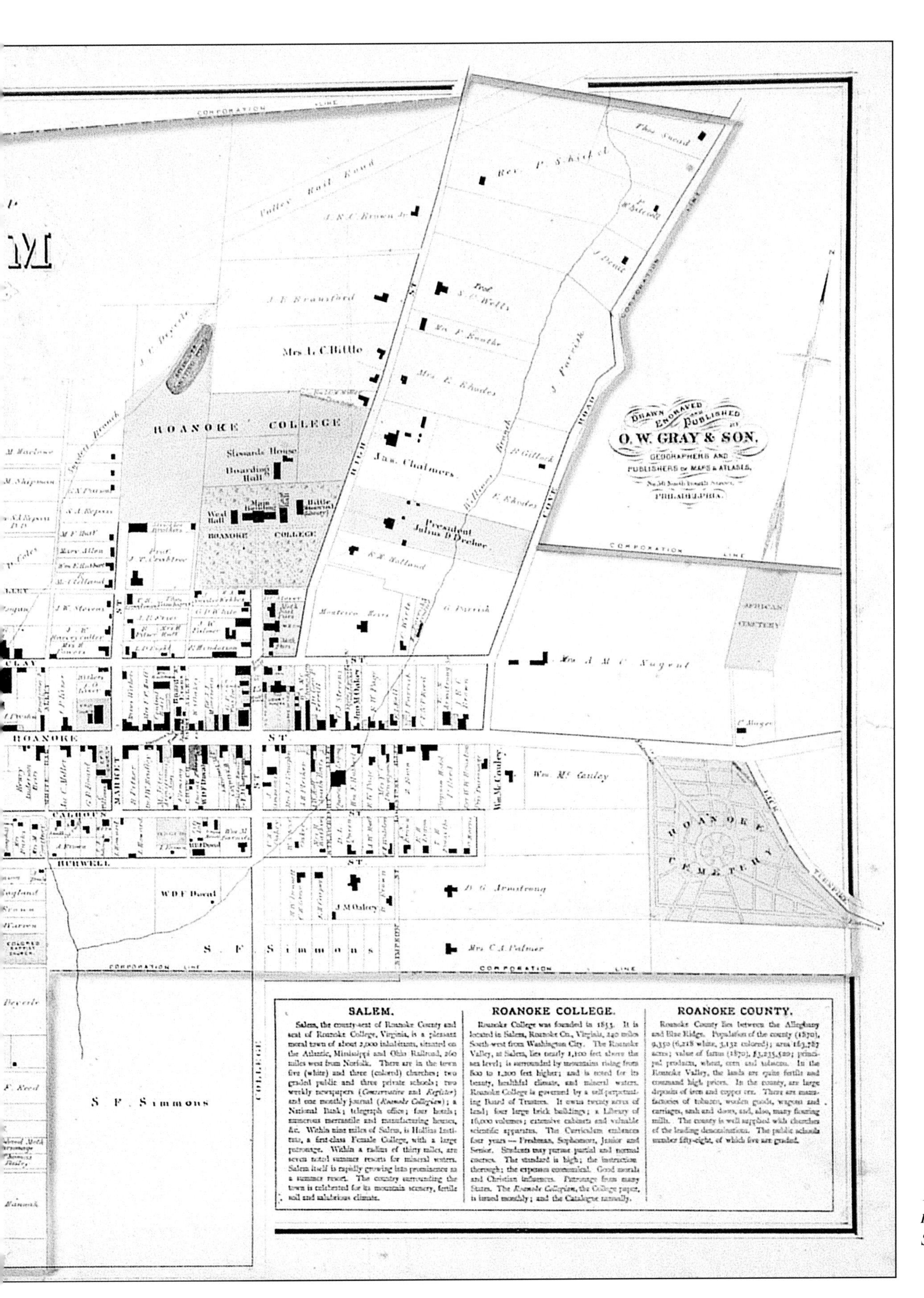

1883 map of Salem.

This mill on Mason's Creek operated from 1845 to the 1930s under the name Garst Mill, Salem Mill, Salem Roller Mills, and finally Kesler Mill.

The Pierpont Brickyard in West Salem.

The Salem Machine Company produced these engines—shown before and after years of use.

An 1890s view of town from East Hill.

The Saul home on the corner of the Boulevard and Tennessee Street. Standing in front is Green Adkins, who worked for the Saul family. In the background is (left to right) John Peter Saul, Sr., daughter Lila, wife Lula and son John.

William McCauley, his wife Margaret, and children outside the Elms, their home on East Main. McCauley served as County Clerk of Court, Roanoke College English Professor, and the foremost local historian.

One of the most spectacular homes in the area was Fort Lewis, west of Salem. Built in 1822 by the White family, the stately mansion took its name from the colonial fort that had stood on the property. The Whites owned Fort Lewis until the early 20th century. Later it belonged to the family of Hollywood star John Payne. The house burned in 1949.

A mill on the Fort Lewis property.

Fort Lewis mansion, side view.

Train passing through West Salem.

The Old Town Hall at the corner of College and Clay.

The Rev. David Bush and his wife Evangeline. Bush pastored Salem Methodist Church and often appeared in the pulpit with his canine assistant, Doc.

This composite photo from the 1920s shows four of Salem's leading churches of the 19th century.

First Baptist Church, the primary African American church on Water Street (now Broad), still retains its original sanctuary.

Pastor Benjamin Fox led First Baptist for ten years before leaving to establish Shiloh Baptist nearby.

South Salem Christian Church Sunday School, 1897.

College Lutheran Church, established 1852, is shown here in the 1920s, just before the building was replaced by Farmer's National Bank. The church moved south on College Avenue to a new sanctuary in 1922.

Salem Town Band, 1890.

Salem Oddfellows Lodge, outside of the old Tabernacle building near College Avenue. On the left side of the front row is Town Sergeant Jacob Frier. Having lost an eye in the Civil War, Frier is almost always pictured in profile.

Academy Street school soon after its construction in 1890, before the adjacent building was erected in 1895 to be used as a high school.

A typical Roanoke College student prank of the late 19th century: putting "Old Man Huff's" wagon atop the Administration Building.

Roanoke College front quad showing Miller Hall, the Administration Building, Trout Hall, and Bittle Library. By 1902 a third floor had been built on top of the Ad Building.

A horse race, or possibly some sort of military procession, in front of the old Hotel Salem.

An oxcart trudges along a dusty Main Street.

When the United States and Spain went to war in 1898, Salem boys were again quick to volunteer. A local militia unit had been formed in 1890, and it was now mustered into the US Army as the Jeff Davis Rifles under command of Judge Wingfield Griffin (front row left, with hands on hips). The unit, with 113 men (24 from Salem), was sent to Florida but saw no action during its seven-month deployment.

Another Griffin made his mark at sea. Thomas Dillard Griffin, who was too young to fight in the Civil War with his four brothers, entered the Naval Academy in 1872. During the Spanish-American War, he was placed aboard the USS Brooklyn. *Griffin was with Admiral Dewey in Manila Bay and rose to the rank of Commodore (one of the last men to hold that rank before it was abolished). He retired in 1911, only to be recalled to serve in World War I. Griffin died in Annapolis in 1938.*

Salem's earliest photographer, and one of the most important in Virginia of his day, was Adam Plecker. Settling in town with his wife Margaret, Plecker operated his "Mammoth Photograph Gallery" on Main Street and also ran a traveling studio out of a boxcar wagon. His works varied from the standard studio shots to the less usual images, such as this ghostly woman on a pedestal.

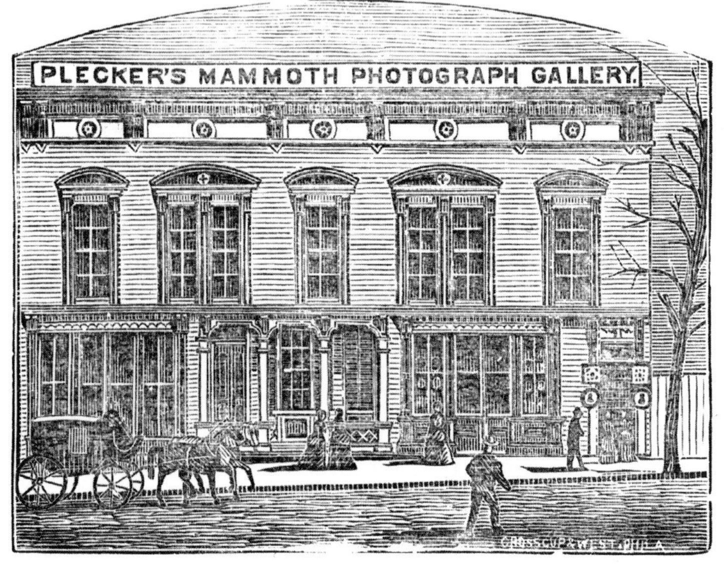

A. H. PLECKER, Salem, Va.

DUPLICATES OF THIS PHOTO. CAN BE HAD BY APPLYING THROUGH THE MAIL OR OTHERWISE.

Adam Plecker.

The Pleckers in a sleigh. Note the stylized studio backdrop.

Margaret Plecker.

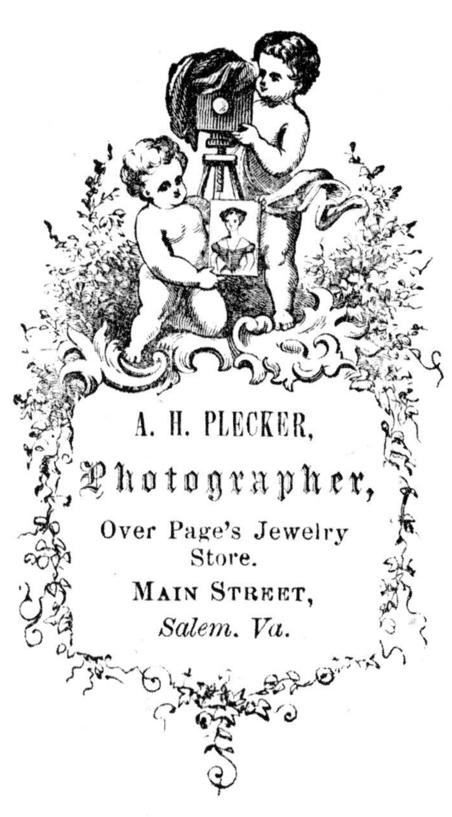

One of Plecker's many backmarks.

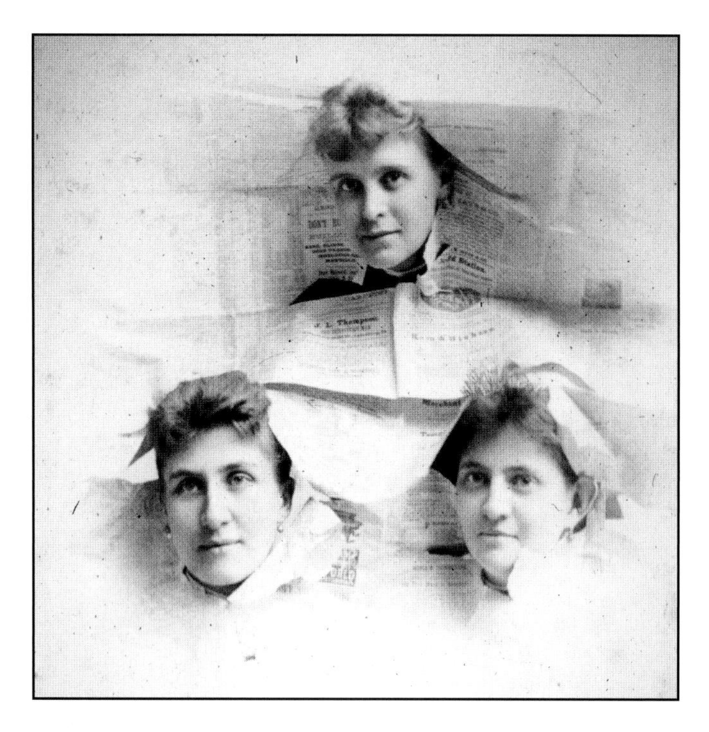

Plecker used a range of settings for his studio work, as seen in these unidentified photographs. The shot of women sticking their heads through newspaper may have been a stage in Plecker's creation of some sort of special effect.

General R. E. Lee and Traveler,
taken from Life in 1866 by A. H. Plecker

Probably the best-known work of Adam Plecker was his 1866 photograph of Robert E. Lee in civilian dress astride his horse Traveler. This image, colorized here for a postcard, sold so well that Plecker's 1929 obituary mentioned it.

Maury Brothers photograph of gypsies passing through Salem.

When Plecker moved to Lynchburg to continue business about 1877, he turned the Salem studio over to his nephews (and adopted sons) Thomas and Charles Maury, who continued the family tradition for years afterwards.

Chapter 3

This 1890s anonymous painting immediately brings to mind Edward Beyer's similar view. The artist painted from the same East Hill location but saw a town that had grown considerably in the intervening 35 years. This painting hung in the Bank of Salem for many years and was given to the Salem Museum in 1998 by First Union Bank.

Vanished Salem 2
Elizabeth College

Top and left: Celebrating George Washington's birthday, 1918.

Previous page: Elizabeth College Main Building by night; a line of "Lizzies."

Above: Clowning around between classes.

EC students eating snow.

At the water pump.

The Elizabeth College Library.

With the arrival of Roanoke College in 1847, Salem became known as a center of education and refinement for young men, especially young Lutheran men, from throughout the nation and around the world. But what of the women? Other than the occasional "special student" with permission to take classes there and even receive a certificate (but not a diploma), there was no place in Salem for young ladies to pursue a higher education.

Until 1912.

A confluence of factors brought a women's college to Salem in that year. In nearby Marion, a Lutheran women's junior college was experiencing financial problems. Two Virginia synods met in Roanoke to discuss relocating Marion College and considered a number of possible sites; Salem, with its reputation for exemplary Lutheran education, won out. Marion College, incidentally, refused the invitation to close and remained in operation until 1967.

The site chosen in Salem was Sherwood, the estate originally part of Andrew Lewis' Richfield plantation and later owned by Nathaniel Burwell. Most recently it had been owned by Robert "Country Bob"

The cast of Shakespeare's As You Like It.

The set of The Florist Shop.

Logan, a Burwell descendant. The new trustees initially settled on the name Oakmont for the school, but after less than a month changed it to Roanoke Woman's College.

Classes began in October of 1912, at first in the old Belmont Hotel on the Boulevard until the campus facilities were completed. Forty-two students joined a small faculty and President John Peery (a Roanoke graduate) to form the college community.

RWC was barely off the ground when a spectacular opportunity led to another name change. In 1915, Dr. Charles E. King approached the school with an offer. King was founder and president of Elizabeth College in Charlotte, NC, a small Lutheran school specializing in musical education, which was on the verge of closing. He suggested a merger of the two schools. King would donate to the Salem school much of his faculty, the library, furnishings, pianos, art supplies, science equipment, and the name Elizabeth. He would also help raise an endowment for the school. It was too good an offer to reject, and the deal was made. Amidst great excitement, Roanoke Woman's College became Elizabeth College.

Elizabeth College Dramatic Club

"The Taming of the Shrew"

Town Hall

Saturday Evening, June 1, 1918

8:15 o'clock

A Midsummer Night's Dream

WILLIAM SHAKESPEARE

PRESENTED BY

Elizabeth College Dramatic Club

MISS DAISY BUCHANAN, DIRECTOR

SATURDAY, JUNE 3, 1916 8:15 P. M.

"Soul of the age!
Th' applause! delight! the wonder of our stage!
My Shakespeare, rise!
Thou art a monument, without a tomb,
And art alive still, while thy book doth live,
And we have wits to read, and praise to give."

DRAMATIS PERSONÆ

Theseus, duke of Athens — Ollie Sanders
Egeus, father to Hermia — Pauline Graham
Lysander, betrothed to Hermia — Anita Rittenberg
Demetrius, once suitor to Helena, now in love with Hermia — Ellen Douglas Jones
Philostrate, master of the revels to Theseus — Stella Hammond
Hippolyta, queen of the Amazons, betrothed to Theseus — Ethel Meek
Hermia, Daughter to Egeus, betrothed to Lysander — Evangeline Killian

Ruth Cooper
Mary Feller
Stella Davis
Aminee Woods
Nello Gose
Marian Miller
Carrie Knipp
Louise Denit
Lucy Rice
Pauline Knee
Elsie Huffard
Blanche Cooper
Dorothy Jones
Ellen Vaught
Maria Cooper, and Catherine Jones
ood near it.

Persons in the Play

Baptista, a rich gentleman of Padua	Ruth Copenhaver
Petruchio, a suitor to Katherine	Ethel Saner
Hortensio, husband to Bianca	Alverta Greever
SERVANTS TO BAPTISTA	
Pedro	Francis Miller
Biondello	Beulah Geil
SERVANTS OF PETRUCHIO	
Grumio	Mary Feller
Walter	Louise Swanson
Nathaniel	Louise Gieschen
Gregory	Francis Miller
Gabriel	Georgia Kinzer
A Music Master	Louise Carr
Katherine, the Shrew	Jean Schroth
Bianca, her sister	Louise Swanson
Curtis, Petruchio's housekeeper	Louise Carr
A Tailor	Carrie Knipp

Scene

Act I. A Hall in Baptista's house in Padua.
Act II. Scene I. The same as Act I.
Scene II. Hall of Petruchio's country house.
Act III The same as the last.

Programs from EC Drama Club presentations.

A maypole celebration on campus.

Basketball and tennis teams.

Field Hockey "Orange" Team, 1919.

Wading between classes.

Trip to McAfee's Knob.

"Dear Old Betsy" enjoyed a happy but all too short existence. Music, athletics, and day trips to nearby sites of interest enlivened the ladies' studies. Concern with the World War and the shortages that resulted cast only a minor pall over the campus. No one could know that worse was to come.

On the morning of December 22, 1921, while the students were home on Christmas break, a fire erupted in Elizabeth's "seemingly indestructible" Main Hall. Faulty electric wires were cited as the cause, but it was rumored that thieves had looted the building and torched it to conceal their crime. Whatever the cause, the results were devastating. The building was utterly destroyed. The next morning, one Roanoke professor pronounced Elizabeth's epitaph: "Born in a fight, died in a fire."

Still, there was a semester to complete, and hopes ran high. Proclaimed one student: "Elizabeth is not dead! Her spirit still lives on in spite of her cremation. We, her loyal orphans, come back—not to the old gray building on the hill, but to the hospitable homes of the townspeople of Salem, where we are made to feel that the loss of our college, devastating

Graduates, probably the class of 1916, with a flower chain.

An EC grad heads out (in the words of one of her classmates) "into the cold, cruel world."

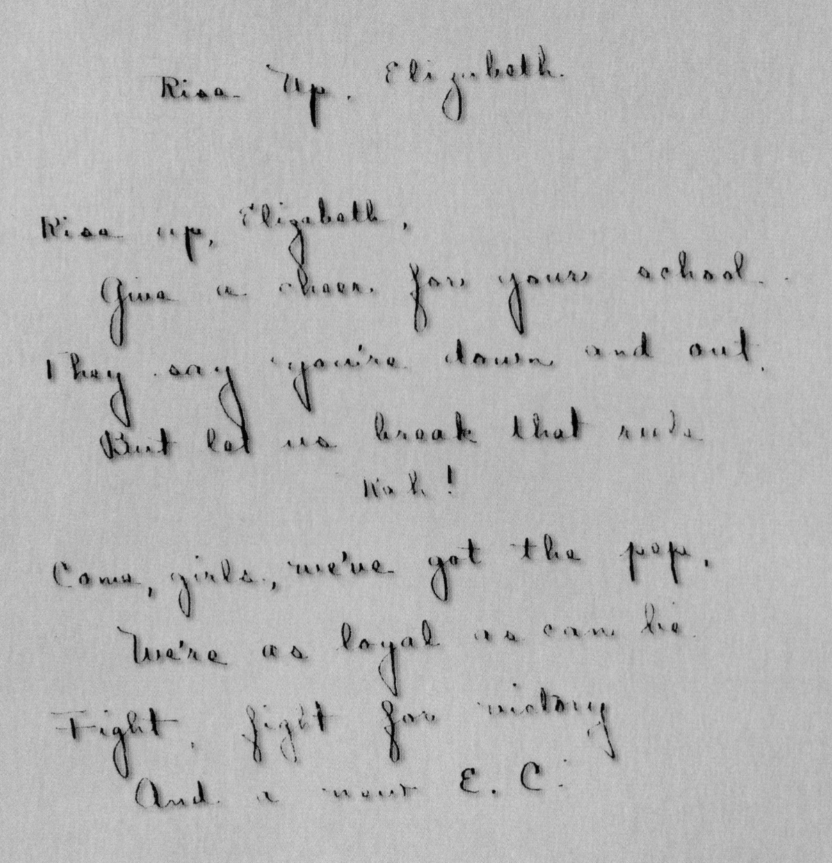

Rise Up, Elizabeth.

Rise up, Elizabeth,
Give a cheer for your school.
They say you're down and out,
But let us break that rule
Rah!
Come, girls, we've got the pep,
We're as loyal as can be
Fight, fight for victory
And a new E. C.

After the fire, students explore the ruins of their beloved school.

as it is, is not irreparable." Indeed, homes became dormitories, and classroom space was provided by Salem High School and Roanoke College. "(F)or the first time in the history of EC, High Street and Roanoke College campus are not forbidden territory!" wrote a diarist.

But this phoenix was not to rise from her ashes for very long. Although college backers were optimistic, the two synods which oversaw the school ordered the termination of Elizabeth College in March of 1922, and EC reluctantly closed.

The property was afterwards turned over to the Lutheran Children's Home, which built new facilities and operated there for many years. Much of the land was eventually deeded to Roanoke College, and in 1996 passed on to the City of Salem in exchange for some property closer to campus. A debate over developing the land and a proposed water tower there brought the name Elizabeth back into the headlines late in the century; however, by then few were left who remembered when "Dear Old Betsy" flourished majestically high on a hill east of town. ❦

4

To Salem Then We Sing Our Praise

1902-1952

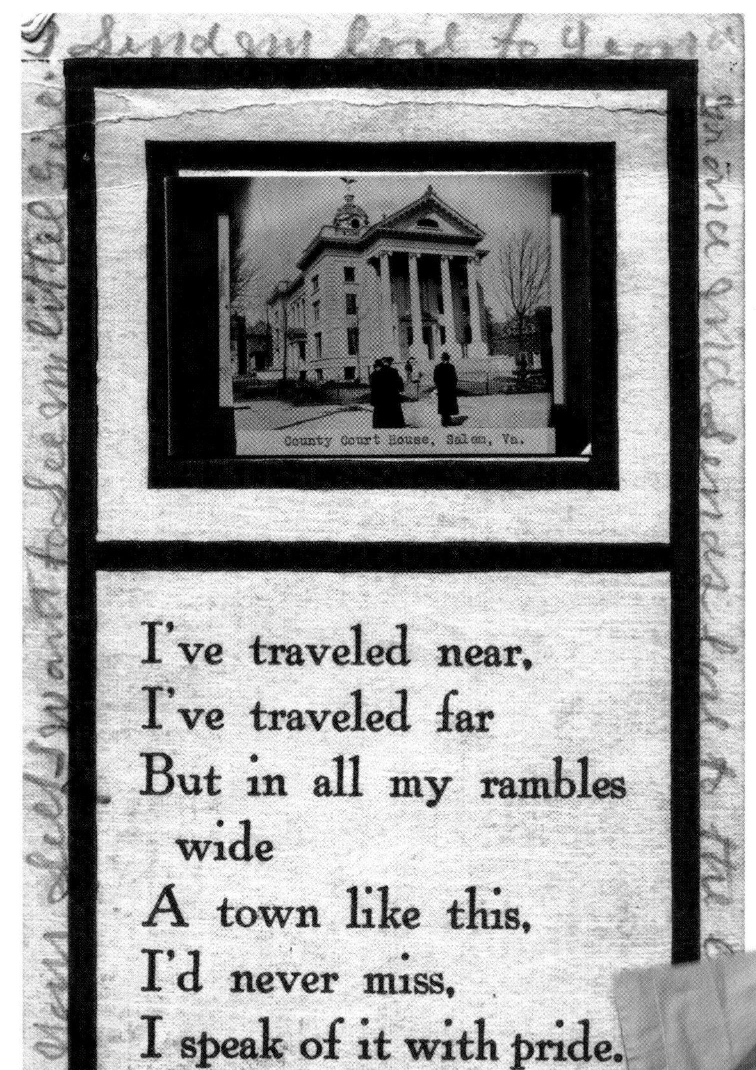
County Court House, Salem, Va.
I've traveled near,
I've traveled far
But in all my rambles
wide
A town like this,
I'd never miss,
I speak of it with pride.

Postcard showing Roanoke County's second courthouse, erected in 1910 on the site of its predecessor. Note that the clock and Confederate statue have yet to be erected.

Campfire Girls uniform worn by Mary Preston.

Previous page: Local ladies wait on tracks near Mason Creek to catch the train to Bennett Springs.

The age of the automobile dawned in Salem, as it did around the country, during the early 1900s, but folks were slow to take to the new-fangled machines. In one early incident, an itinerant car salesman tried to show Salemites a car's potential for speed—only to be told by the mayor to "go and sin no more." The Salem Automobile Company, one of the town's first dealerships, was not formed until seven years later in 1912.

Salem's third half-century would prove to be her most tumultuous yet—and her most exciting. Two world wars, the Depression, questions of racial harmony and other turmoils were balanced against amazing technological change and exhilarating new opportunities. But through it all Salem met every change and challenge with grace and her own unique charm.

The first years of the 20th century were perhaps the most care-free on record. Salemites enjoyed costume parties, silent film showings in the Town Hall, ice skating, and concerts by the town band. Romance and elopements crowded more serious news out of the papers. Youngsters had new opportunities to socialize, learn skills, and contribute to the community through the formation of a Salem Boy Scout troop in 1911, followed by the Campfire Girls in 1912. When streetcar lines extended to Lake Spring, the town's first and only public park, residents from throughout the valley flocked to enjoy summer days near the picturesque ponds.

Meanwhile, the appearance of Salem began to alter. Model T Fords puttered along newly paved streets, changing the way Salemites worked and traveled. A new courthouse graced Main Street in 1910. Fabulous houses, such as Longwood and the Shickel home (today's John M. Oakey & Sons funeral parlor), rose from the ashes of the deflated boom.

Another early photo of the Roanoke County courthouse.

Shirley Spurlock, a former slave of Nathaniel Burwell, purchased land in Salem three years after the end of the Civil War. He later moved to Government Hill, which was then in Roanoke County and therefore outside Salem's segregated districts. Spurlock served as the butler at Longwood (just south of Government Hill). He is shown here with two of his grandchildren, Sadie Arletta Morrison on his knee and her sister (unidentified).

Cow loose on Roanoke College campus.

This is not to say that these buoyant years were without controversy. The matter of cows roaming free on the streets had crowds of incensed citizens flocking to town meetings, petitions in hand. On the pro-cow side, it was argued that outlawing free-roaming cows was unfair to poor families who needed the milk, but could not afford to provide an attendant to herd the animals to pasture daily. Anti-cow groups countered that "the leading streets of our town... (had been turned into) veritable 'barnyards'" and the expense of fencing should fall upon the cow-owners, not their cow-less neighbors. On February 1, 1913, after years of contention and three different referenda, an ordinance to prohibit livestock on the streets without an attendant took effect—and Salem's days of free-roaming cows were over.

An equally spirited debate over the establishment of local pool rooms inspired much impassioned rhetoric around town. Church leaders and concerned citizens led efforts to prohibit the creation of what they deemed a moral "calamity" which would cause "the cluck of the ivory balls (to become) music far more sweet to (youngsters') ears than the voices of mother and father around the home fireside." One perturbed citizen was quoted in the newspaper as remarking, "There are some folks who are bound to play pool and drink likker, and I say to them, go on to Roanoke where you belong!"

Neighborhoods were not the only things segregated during the first half of the 20th century. This is believed to be the African-American Roanoke Machine Works baseball team of the Norfolk and Western Railroad, coached by Salemite LeRoy Duckwilder. Many local industries sponsored both black and white teams.

Alongside these debates, more serious issues of racial segregation districts arose. When a "white only" residential district was defined in a traditionally black neighborhood, African-American citizens responded with consternation at the cramped quarters allotted by the new ordinance. Lawyer John P. Saul, Jr., was

Salem prepares to welcome WWI veterans home with a parade of soldiers down Main Street.

WWI soldiers in front of Sections at Roanoke College.

hired to plead the case to council and Salem's African-American district was soon enlarged.

When America entered the First World War in 1917, Salem was quick to respond. Doughboys enlisted, while folks on the homefront rolled bandages and sold Liberty Bonds. By the end of the "War to End All Wars," 15 of Salem's sons had given their lives. Almost as devastating was the flu epidemic of 1918, which claimed 14 local lives.

Despite these losses, the community rallied and Salem hosted elaborate celebrations to welcome soldiers home on July 5, 1919, as reported by the *Roanoke Times*:

> *Thousands came here today to take part in the big Fourth of July Celebration which began at ten o'clock this morning with a big parade from Lake Spring to the Roanoke College campus. The parade was led by the "Victory Band," preceded by the colors borne aloft by an army motorcycle. Then came the marching column of returned soldiers followed by Confederate veterans in automobiles and twenty army motorcycles with side cars bearing the young ladies who served the service men's luncheon at noon. The remainder of the parade was made of marching children from orphanages, a number of splendidly decorated floats and automobiles.*

WWI welcome home parade. Salem High School's float, shown here, won the first place award of $25, which the winners decided to put toward the school's auditorium fund.

This post office on College Avenue was built in 1907 at the urging of new postmaster Wingfield Griffin, who served until 1910. Constructed for the government by W.B. Dillard and J.S. Persinger, this building remained the site for the Salem office until 1923.

Interior view of the 1907 post office. Notice the portrait of Teddy Roosevelt (who appointed Griffin as postmaster) on the wall.

Like the rest of the nation, Salem enjoyed a post-war boom. The twenties were a decade of considerable progress for the town. The first government-built post office opened on Main Street, and several new commercial buildings were erected. Many of the most positive advancements were brought about at the urging of the Salem Woman's Club, dedicated to the betterment of the community's health and culture. The group worked to establish a community nurse, place trash receptacles on Main Street, and institute health regulations for ice cream parlors (which previously only rinsed their spoons between uses, instead of washing them with hot water and soap).

Pride in the maturing community was expressed by Constance Stearns' winning entry for Town Song in 1918:

To Salem then we sing our praise;
Let echoes ring throughout our days.
O dear old town that we adore
Live in our hearts for evermore!

Post office staff around 1935 in front of Salem's first government-built facility, which operated on the northeast corner of Market and Main from 1923 until 1985.

DEDICATION OF VETERAN'S HOSPITAL ROANOKE, VA. Oct. 19-1934
PRESIDENT FRANKLIN. D. ROOSEVELT MAKING PRINCIPAL ADDRESS

One of Salem's biggest days occurred on October 19, 1934, when Franklin Delano Roosevelt arrived to dedicate the new Veteran's Administration Facility east of town. Schools and offices closed early to allow hundreds of Salemites to watch the president whirl through Salem on his way to the hospital grounds. Here his car passes in front of Andrew Lewis High School.

Salem High School was located in this Broad Street building from 1912 until a devastating fire in 1931. The renovated Broad Street school was used as an elementary school from 1933 until 1977. In 1983, it was converted into Salem's City Hall.

Other substantive advantages accrued from a change in local governance. In 1922, Salem adopted the Council/ Manager form of town government. This system—pioneered just up the road in Staunton—turned management of a municipality over to a supervisor to administer the day-to-day operations with an expert hand. Under the first town manager, John Broome, Salem established better fire fighting facilities and equipment, new municipal offices, improved streets with street lights, and an adequate water supply. This laudable progress was slowed by the Stock Market crash in 1929, but by then Salem had become a modern community.

As the Depression gripped the nation, Salem fared better than most communities. Although welfare rolls exploded, jobs remained relatively plentiful and secure. The construction of a new Veterans Hospital east of Salem created jobs, and brought President Franklin Roosevelt to visit in October 1934. More paved roads, more automobile dealerships and new talking movie theaters marked Salem's transition to the modern world. The town's first public library building opened in 1937.

The question of school facilities came to the forefront in the 1930s. A fire in the old Broad Street high school in 1931 necessitated the construction of a new building. Andrew Lewis High School opened for the 1933-34 school year. Soon after, a drive began to replace the woefully inadequate African-American Training School on Water Street. After much lobbying and debate over a site, Carver School opened in 1940 and

With a Civilian Pilot Training Program in place as early as 1939, Roanoke College was teeming with preparations during World War II. Here recruiters swear in a new batch of soldiers in front of the gym; aviation cadets train on the football field (note silhouettes of Hitler and Mussolini on the climbing board); and both Army and Navy aviation students scatter across the back quad.

Sam Good, shown here sitting in Hitler's chair soon after the fall of Berlin, came to Roanoke College through the GI Bill. He later worked as an administrator and teacher at the College for over thirty years.

The "Big Parade" on August 16, 1952, featured Sesquicentennial Queen Judy Hollady and members of her court, Minnie Barnet Cadd, Barbara Green, Peggy Layman, Marie Mabes, Betty Paxton, Betty St. Clair, and Mary Alice Woods.

Sesquicentennial beauties at Longwood mansion.

The crowning of Sesquicentennial Queen Judy Hollady opened the historical pageant "The Salem Story" nightly from August 11 to 16, 1952 at the Municipal Ball Park (now Kiwanis Field).

was hailed as one of the finest schools for African American students in the South.

In 1941, Salem again went to war, and over four years 4500 Roanoke County men and women would serve in uniform. At home, Salem played an unexpectedly active role in WWII. An Indiana Street garage housed German prisoners of war who worked for local farmers, Roanoke College sponsored a pilot training program, and the Salem Foundry machined casings used in developing the atomic bomb. When the war ended, Salem celebrated with the rest of the nation and mourned her 43 sons who paid the ultimate price.

Local men would again be called to defend freedom in 1950, this time in Korea. Members of an area Marine Reserve unit, the 16th Engineer Company, were called to active duty in 1950. Many served at the horrific Battle of the Chosin Reservoir.

1952 marked a milestone for Salem: her Sesquicentennial. A festive parade, religious observances, and the extravagant historical drama "The Salem Story,"

The Sesquicentennial.

with a cast of 500, marked the town's 150th birthday. Salem had another reason to celebrate that year: local boy Rusty Gwaltney won the national championship in marbles.

In 1902, Salem was horse-drawn carriages, candle-lit parlors, dirt roads and wandering cows. By 1952, she was automobiles, television, ten-cent payphones and nearly 7,000 spirited citizens. In less than the average life span, more had changed than anyone could have imagined. Greater things were on the horizon. ❦

Scenes from the Sesquicentennial Parade.

Queen Judy Hollady heads home after Sesquicentennial celebrations.

Chapter 4

1924 ariel view of Salem.

1924 ariel view of Roanoke College.

MAIN STREET. SALEM, VA.

Salem's Kiwanis Club was formed in 1921 to promote the mission "We Build." In addition to focusing their efforts on civic improvements, the Club produced these sepia-toned postcards in the 1920s to advance the image of Salem as a modern town.

LANGHORNE HOME. SALEM, VA.

BAPTIST ORPHANAGE. SALEM, VA.

McVITTY HOME. SALEM, VA.

Twelve O'clock Knob from Court
House Dome, Salem, Va.

Water Street looking North,
Salem, Va.

Interior of Court Room,
New Court House, Salem, Va.

N. & W. Passenger Station,
Salem, Va.

SUMMER GARDEN AT REAR OF SALEM THEATRE, SALEM, VA.

Main Street, Salem, Va.

STREET SCENE - SALEM, VA.

These two views of Salem—one looking west early in the century and the other looking east around the 1940s—show the radical changes that took place on Salem's Main Street.

Beloved to generations of Salemites was Longwood. their very own castle. Longwood was built in 1904 by Thomas Henry Cooper, president of Colonial Bank & Trust, Cooper Silica Glass Company, and his family's West Virginia coal concern. The mansion was rumored to cost $100,000 and featured gracious elegance from the parquet floors to the orange tiled roof.

Longwood blueprints.

Miniature horse and carriage in front of Longwood.

The Cooper family at Longwood gardens.

Children on the Longwood lawn.

Baby's first steps outside the mansion.

In 1942, with the death of Cooper's wife Mary, Longwood was purchased at auction by the town of Salem and used as a community center. Here, the Kiwanis Club meets at Longwood in 1951.

Stairway sculpture from Longwood.

The house burned in 1968 while undergoing renovations, and was deemed beyond repair. The only surviving structure was the adjacent Carriage House, which in 2002 was adapted to serve the Salem-Roanoke County Chamber of Commerce.

Frank C. Wiley, Lawson Wiley, and Mrs. W. T. Younger on the east porch of the Younger Home. The house, which was torn down in 1935, was located where Salem Public Library now stands on Main Street.

The dining room of this home on Union Street originally served as an office for one of Salem's early brickyards. It was later renovated as a residence and is shown here in the early 20th century.

On the right is D.B. Strouse, a lawyer and entrepreneur turned evangelist, in front of his impressive Broad Street home.

This cabin on Franklin Street remains a family residence today.

The original portion of "Boxwood" was built in the early 1800s by judge and entrepreneur Green B. Board. The Main Street home was torn down in 1963.

Baptist preacher Frank P. Robertson moved to Salem with his family in 1905 and built this house on Red Lane, where it still stands today.

1923 Christmas party at the S. H. McVitty home, Ridgewood.

Mary and Dorothy McCauley in back yard of the McCauley home on East Main.

Richard Garst with slingshot.

Hank Bellinger at play on Government Hill.

Ready for a swim, these girls (all members of an informal "cooking school") gathered in the backyard of High Street's Roselawn. Harriett Stokes, whose painting of Salem is on the cover of this book, is standing on the far right.

Circus passing through town in the early 1900s.

Frank Cameron Wiley, one of the early organizers of Salem's horse shows.

Homecoming Celebration on July 4, 1930, at the Roanoke County courthouse. Boy Scouts Edgar Yates, John Butler, and Edward Walker patrol the streets.

Academy Street school, built in 1890.

Students on the steps of Academy Street school in early 1900s.

1909 graduating class at Academy Street school. Principal Lucy T. Jones is on the top step.

Salem High School Drama Club, 1907.

Academy Street students show off their birdhouses (above) and enjoy a bit of exercise (below).

South Salem School on Mount Regis in the early 1900s.

Roanoke County Training students exercise in the school yard.

Students gather on the steps of the courthouse to protest the dismissal of Salem High School principal A. M. Bruce in 1929.

Salem's new high school, named in honor of Revolutionary War hero Andrew Lewis, opened for white students in 1933.

George Washington Carver School opened for African-American students in 1940.

1940s Carver students Anderson "Texas" Williams, Jimmy Whitlock, Howard "Chutie" Jackson, Raymond "Jenks" Joiner, and Ralph Dent on Water Street.

Salem High enjoyed Virginia basketball championships in 1916, 1917, and 1918.

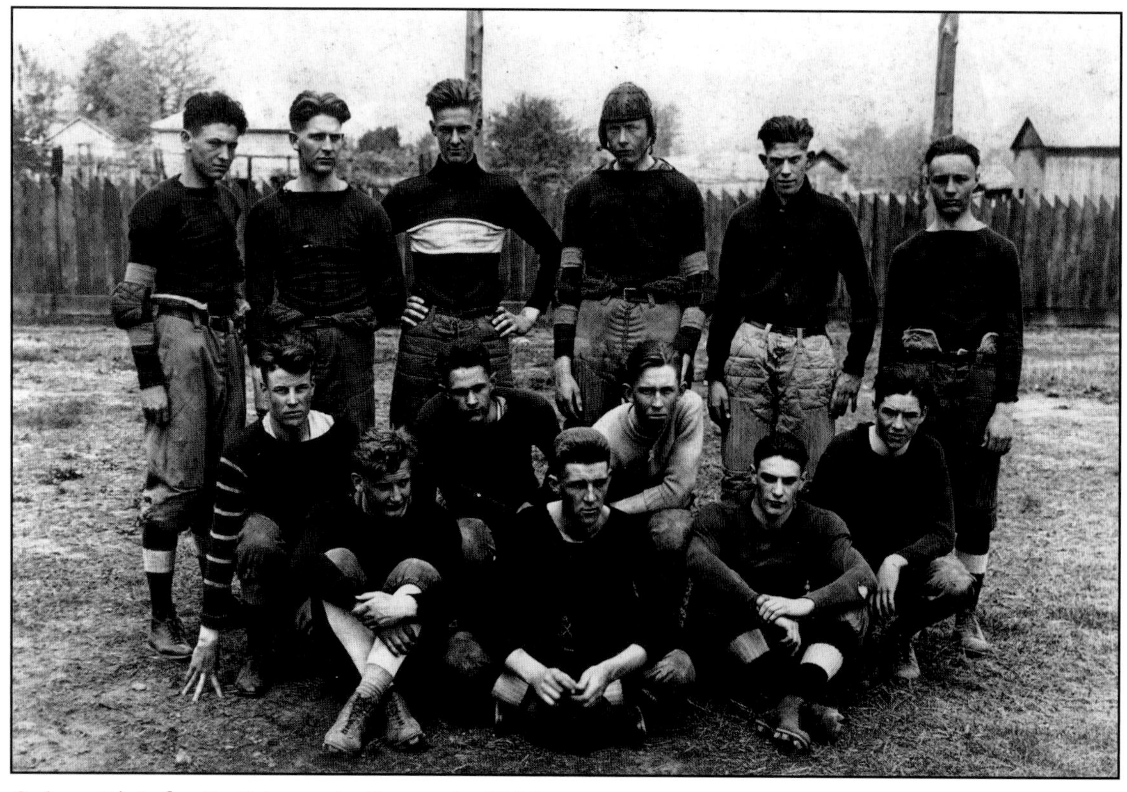

Salem High football team in the early 1900s.

Salem girls' and boys' ball teams.

Roanoke College campus after a storm.

Roanoke College campus life in the teens and twenties.

"Baby Day" at Salem Baptist Church, October 14, 1923.

Young People's Choir of Salem Baptist Church, 1935.

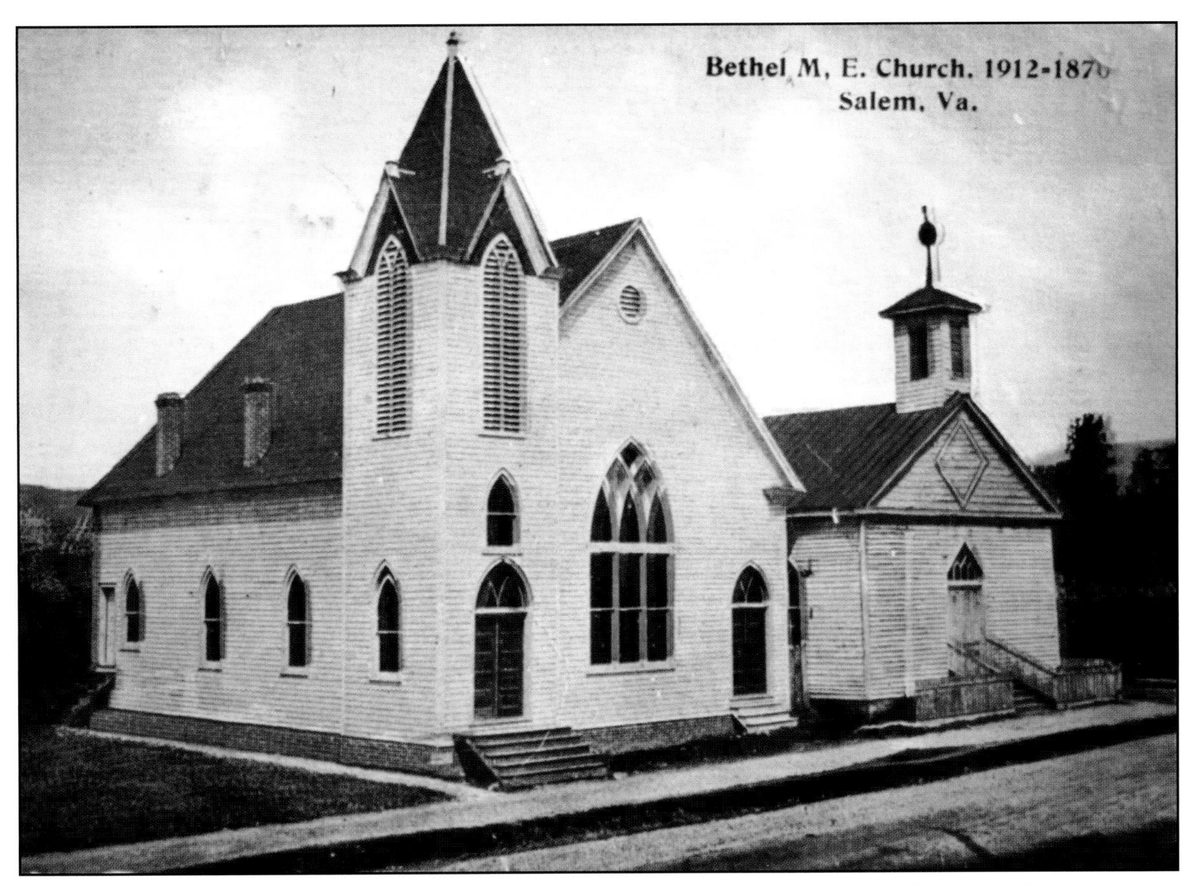

Organized in 1868, Bethel A. M. E. Church on Water Street moved into this building about 1912.

Shiloh Baptist Church was formed when longtime First Baptist minister B. F. Fox led a split of his congregation in 1896. The building shown here was constructed in 1911.

West Main Street store and residence in the early 1900s.

Perdue Groceries was frequented by Elizabeth College students and locals in the teens.

Salem newsstand and streetcar ticket office run by Warren Moorman, Sr., in the 1920s.

Western Union and OK Realty on Main Street around the 1920s.

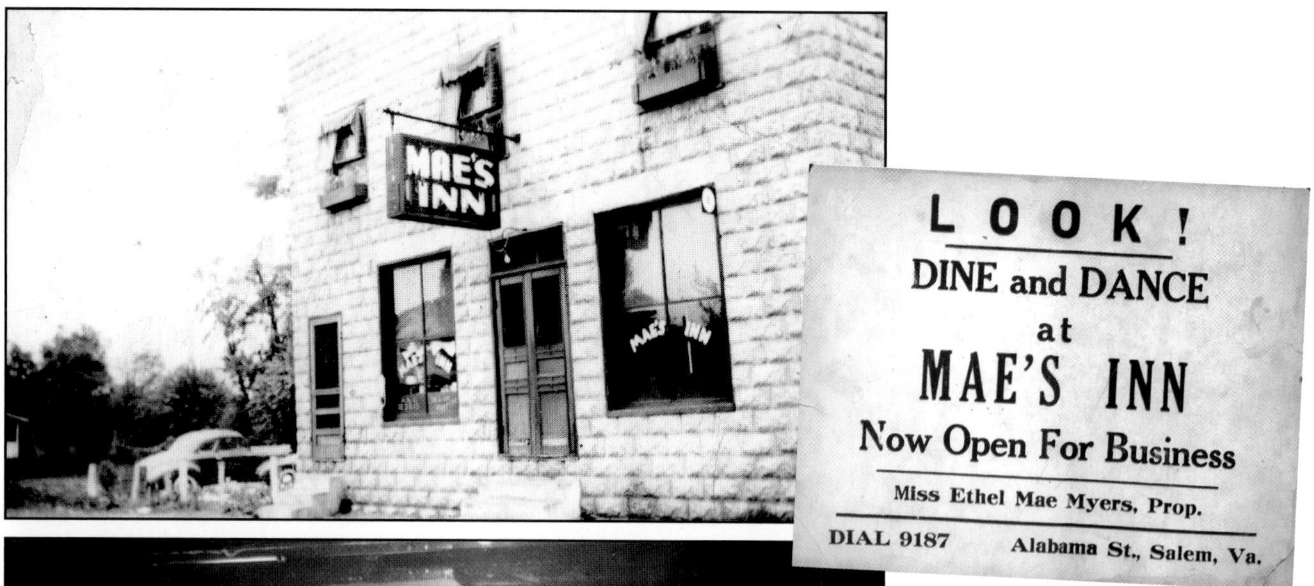

MAE'S INN
LOOK!
DINE and DANCE
at
MAE'S INN
Now Open For Business
Miss Ethel Mae Myers, Prop.
DIAL 9187
Alabama St., Salem, Va.

Ethel Mae Myers operated a restaurant and juke joint for African Americans on Alabama Street in the 1940s. The building later housed Salem Masonic Lodge 120.

Men's Wear store on Main Street.

Goodwin's Store west of Salem.

Exterior and lobby of Hotel Fort Lewis around the 1940s. The hotel, which stood on the southeast corner of Main at Colorado, was built as Williams Hotel in 1851 and subsequently known as American, Central, Lucerne, Duval, Crawford, and Salem. It was demolished in 1974.

The Homestead Hotel on Main Street was operated by Minnie B. Snyder, who started Snyder's Nursing Home in an adjacent building in 1956.

Salem Theatre, built in 1929.

Farmer's National Bank was established in 1871 and remained a fixture of Salem's financial world for more than a century. Originally located on the south side of Main, the bank moved in 1923 to a new building on the corner of College and Main.

The bank logo changed through time, but the bank remained an anchor of Main Street for many years. FNB merged in 1975 with First Virginia Bank.

Clerk Ivan V. Yonce, Sr., is shown here inside a Norfolk and Western railway mail car.

Employees of Salem Foundry and Machine Works.

Workers at the Leas & McVitty Tannery, which was founded in 1812 and came to Salem 1889. S. H. McVitty arrived in 1902 to run the business—the fourth generation of his family to do so. Under his leadership, L&M became a leading supplier of leather. McVitty died in 1967, and the firm was sold a few years later. The new owners planned to phase out operations, but a 1973 fire hastened the tannery's demise.

THE
STORE
HARDWARE

Firehouse and engine, next to the old Town Hall on College Avenue, circa 1920.

1925 volunteer fire fighters.

Taking out the old engine for a spin on College Avenue, 1941.

Town Sergeant E. R. Moore in the backseat.

Salem Police Force in the 1930s.

Police Department, circa 1951.

Formed in 1932 (two years before this photo was taken), Salem's volunteer Rescue Squad claims to be the second oldest in the world, after Roanoke's.

Salem Electric Department, 1944.

Portrait of Charlie Hammitt by Walter Biggs.

Hammitt as model and movie star.

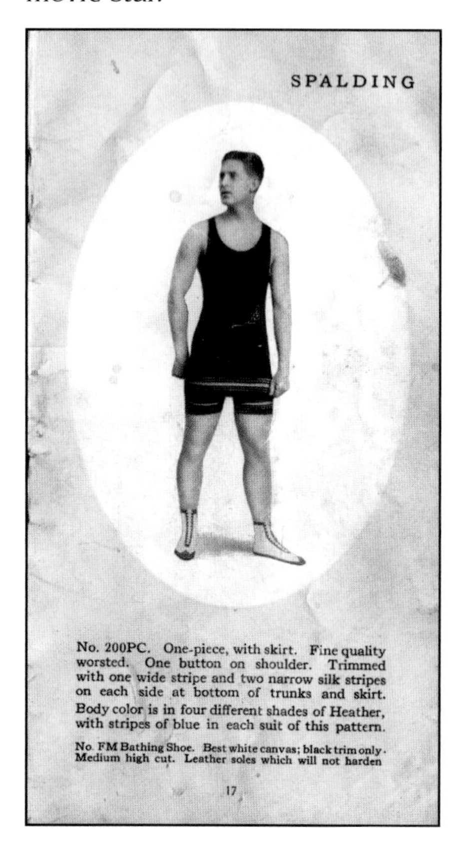

Salem native Charlie Hammitt made a name for himself without speaking a word—as star of a series of silent western films and later as a model. Hammitt's father Charlie Sr., who acted under the stage name Ned Finley, got his son the part of Copperhead Freeman in a series of twelve two-reelers in the late teens. His father's 1920 suicide seemed to have derailed Charlie's film career, but he continued to model. He eventually returned to Salem and worked for the Bank of Salem and Brooks-Byrd Pharmacy. Hammitt stayed in the footlights of local productions for years afterwards. He died in 1975.

Hammitt, the hero in the Copperhead Freeman series, acted under the name "Dick Camp."

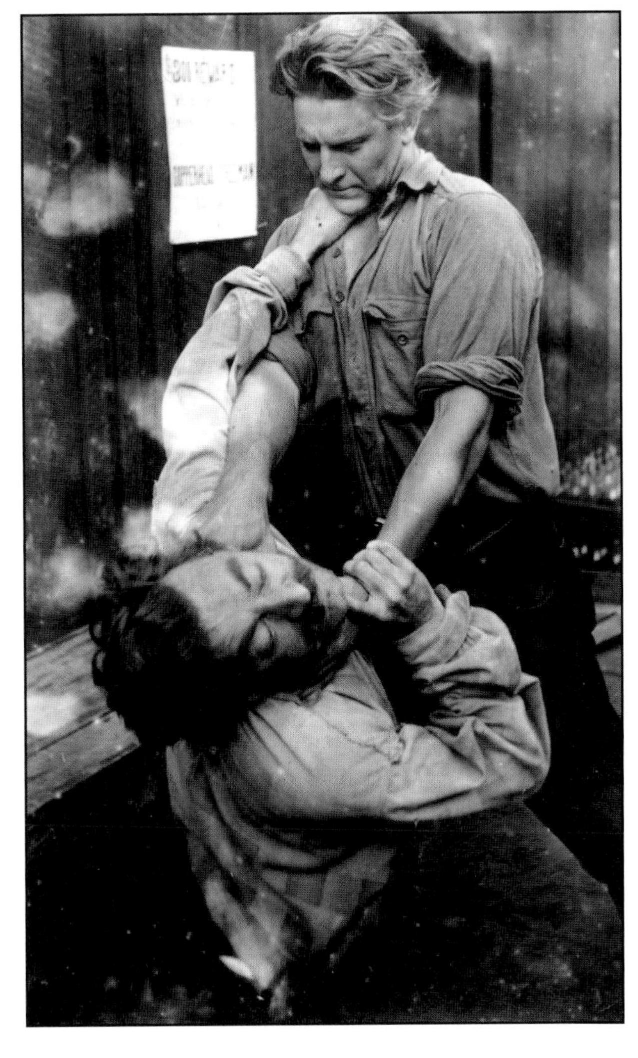

Alfreda Peel (standing) in a theatre production of her play Three Mile Field. *After her death in 1953, all copies of her play were called in by her estate and apparently disappeared.*

Alfreda Marion Peel was one of Salem's most prominent writers and one of the south's most active folklorists. Peel, a teacher by profession, was credited with recording over 2500 mountain ballads and folktales as one of the founders of the Virginia Folklore Society. She is best remembered for her 1947 book Witch in the Mill*; her silhouette illustrations for the book were praised by no less an admirer as Walter Biggs.*

Masie tole Liza to let her cow alone.

The best known artist of the Roanoke Valley was the extraordinary Walter Biggs (seen in a self-portrait at right). Born in Elliston in 1886, Biggs came to Salem as a boy and in his heart never left. After studies at New York's famed Chase School, Biggs became a nationally known illustrator for such magazines as Harper's *and* Ladies Home Journal. *Biggs returned to Salem in the 1950s to care for his ailing mother and sister. Locally, his works featuring local scenes and people—including sensitive portrayals of the denizens of Water Street—are especially prized. Biggs died in 1968.*

The Letter, *currently on display at the Salem Museum, captures the impressionistic style of Biggs' illustrations. For models, Biggs often relied on members of his family, local residents (such as former slave and preacher "Uncle Watt, above") and even himself.*

Katie Dillard of Salem.

The Post House, *near the corner of Market and Main.*

Biggs' sensitive portrayal of African Americans won him much acclaim, and this painting (entitled War News*) was awarded a Gold Medal of Honor by the American Watercolor Society.*

The original Roanoke County courthouse.

Vanished Salem 3

Lakeside

Top left and center right: Swimmers on Lakeside's opening day, July 10, 1920.

LAKESIDE, LARGEST SWIMMING POOL IN THE WORLD. SALEM, VA.

Early scenes from Lakeside Park.

It's a hot summer Friday in Salem, Virginia—pretty much any hot summer Friday around the middle of the 20th century. After breakfast, hundreds of visitors pour out of cars and buses with suntan lotion and picnic lunches. Each one passes through a turnstile and is tagged with a color-coded charm around the wrist. It won't be long until screams of fear and delight rack the air....

Past dusk a straggler's parade of die-hards wander back to their vehicles. Some are slightly sunburned; others have a queasy greenish glow. They clutch neon-colored stuffed animals, plastic trinkets and balloons as they head home, exhausted but happy.

The next day, it happens all over again.

What, you may ask, could possibly create such a perfect mix of ecstasy and turmoil in the human heart? Well, the Spider for one. And the Slide. And the Flight Through Space. Not to mention the dozens of other rides that found a home in the Valley's beloved Lakeside Amusement Park between the 1920s and 1980s.

Of course, before the rides came one heck of a pool. In 1919, a group of

1924 ariel view of the park, now featuring the Thriller.

investors led by Robert Lee Lynn and H. E. Hogan purchased an orchard at the edge of town for the purpose of operating a "general pleasure resort" known as Lakeside. The name referred to the two million gallon swimming pool that they soon built.

Upon opening, Lakeside's swimming pool was described in the *Salem Times-Register* as quite immense, measuring 300 feet by 125 feet, with an artificial beach surrounding the area and "thousands of electric lights illuminat[ing] the grounds." The pool's pump was advertised to be capable of providing 20,000 gallons of fresh water each hour. Lakeside later claimed to run the world's largest swimming pool.

While the original Lakeside charter called for the pool, athletic fields, and a planned hotel, no mention was made of rides. Yet within a few years, Lakeside had added a "Twirl-around" (Ferris wheel), "Lindy Planes" (named for heroic aviator Charles Lindbergh), pony rides, and other attractions. Probably most popular was a roller coaster known successively as the Thriller, Mountain Speedway, and the Wildcat.

Lakeside became a center of controversy in the

Cupie doll souvenir.

Greyhound from a Lakeside arcade game.

Two of Lakeside's popular rides: the Lindy Planes and the Peanut.

20s when local Judge W. W. Moffett decreed that the pool's opening to "half naked" swimmers on Sunday was detrimental to public morals. The local sheriff disagreed, saying that Lakeside prevented law-breaking, since skinny-dipping along the creeks and Roanoke River had diminished as a result of the pool. The case went all the way to the state Supreme Court, which ruled that Lakeside could remain open on Sundays. Park manager Robert Lynn (also president of Heironimus department store) soon closed the park on Sundays anyway, claiming that he had proven his point but didn't want to offend anyone.

In 1936, Lakeside was purchased by H. L. Roberts, whose family would own the park for the next 45 years. Early on, Roberts considered a radical course of action that fortunately did not pan out. Convinced that the pool was the moneymaker and the rides a waste of space, Roberts tried to convince a movie company to burn down the roller coaster for a film. Luckily for thrill-seekers, Roberts could never find a taker, and the Mountain Speedway kept rolling.

The Roberts were entrepreneurs of clean family fun. Through the years,

Inside Lakeside's Astroliner.

Salem's lion-mouth fountain.

Lakeside mascots Chip, Prissy Skunk and Lord Beaverbrook.

they jealously guarded Lakeside's reputation as a family park. Alcohol was prohibited, disruptive visitors were evicted, and marketing was aimed at families or groups looking for an affordable outing. Unlike most other amusement parks, Lakeside allowed visitors to bring picnic lunches into the park, sacrificing some concession revenue to draw the desired type of crowd. The park also offered cheap no-ride admission tickets to parents who only wanted to watch their children have fun. Church groups, school groups, family reunions, class reunions, and company picnics were also welcomed.

Lakeside was always looking for new and innovative ways to pack in the visitors. Novelty acts such as parachutists, magicians, and even a daredevil who set himself on fire daily were frequently seen at the park. One of the most important draws was music in the summer, and through the years Lakeside was visited by dozens of jazz, rock, and country music celebrities.

After three decades of swimming and summer fun, the Roberts family decided in the late 60s to embark on a $1 million renovation program, replacing virtually everything in a few short

RAIL ROAD
CROSSING

SHOOTING STAR

years. The centerpiece of the new Lakeside was an immense roller coaster, the Shooting Star, which supplanted the old 1920s Thriller. At a cost of some $225,000, the Shooting Star claimed to be the world's fastest roller coaster when it made its first ride in 1968. The Philadelphia Toboggan Coaster Company's legendary John Allen, who has been credited with a renaissance of wooden coaster development in the 60s and 70s, was responsible for the Shooting Star. According to design specs, the Shooting Star was 84 feet tall and 4,120 feet long. It had two trains (red and blue) consisting of four cars per train and carrying six passengers per car. The entire hair-raising experience took approximately 120 seconds—a mere 2 minutes!—from beginning to end. To build it, the coaster required 320,000 board feet of lumber, 19,000 pounds of steel, 1,600 gallons of paint, 7,000 pounds of nails, 14,000 pounds of bolts, and 600 feet of lift chain powered by a Westinghouse 100-horsepower motor.

Meanwhile, the old pool had become unprofitable, a fact many attributed to whites' unwillingness to swim with blacks after integration. Certainly, the grow-

ing number of backyard pools and private clubs also played a role. Following a brief stint as a private pool, Lakeside's colossal concrete lake was unceremoniously filled in to make space for more rides.

In 1981, an era for Lakeside ended when the Roberts family sold their interest in the park to the F. S. Management Company for $3 million dollars. Despite their efforts to remodel the park, the new owners found themselves in a dispute with the City of Salem over admission taxes and were forced to sell. Mountain Park Inc. bought Lakeside in 1984 and initiated another series of renovations. The most noticeable change was an artificial pond for paddle-boating, dubbed Lake Roberts in honor of the family that had made Lakeside what it was.

Many factors have been identified in bringing about the demise of Lakeside. Competition from larger parks in the state, rising costs, and hikes in the minimum wage all took their toll. The disastrous flood of 1985, when Mason Creek made Lakeside's name temporarily accurate, did immense damage. Still, the park reopened after the flood, and even continued to remodel and innovate.

Perhaps the final straw was an accident in which a maintenance worker was killed in 1986 during a test run of the Shooting Star. The resulting lawsuit helped to convince the management that the park was no longer tenable.

Ultimately Lakeside closed for a simpler reason, to which all its complex problems contributed: it had stopped making enough money. Like any business not turning a profit, the gates soon shut. Lakeside closed forever on October 19, 1986.

What became of the rides from Lakeside? Originally, the Shooting Star was to be dismantled and reassembled at Emerald Pointe in North Carolina. Parts of the superstructure and the trains were moved to the new park, but Emerald Pointe went bankrupt before the Shooting Star was reborn. Much of the framework still sits along Mason Creek, the red and white paint peeling. The beams sent to Emerald Pointe were eventually sold for fencing. The cars were sent back to the manufacturer, PTC. The red train was scrapped, but Lakeside's blue train was sold and still runs at Sea Mist Park in Myrtle Beach. The Frontier Railroad train is still in use at Busch Gar-

LAKESIDE
PARK

dens, and other rides seem to have been sold overseas.

The *Roanoke Times* printed an epitaph for Lakeside on Oct. 22, 1986: "Just as children won't part with toys they've outgrown, the Roanoke Valley didn't want to lose Lakeside.... An amusement park is one of the few places where children and adults can relate on the same level. Kids are free to act like kids, and so are adults. Without Lakeside, there will be a long drive to put a child on a merry-go-round for the first time.... The valley now has one less place where people of any age can be young."

But Lakeside lives on in memories of speed, cotton candy, and carousel music on hot summer nights. ❦

Doodles the Duck.

5

There Will Always Be a Salem

1952-2002

The General Electric Plant under construction.

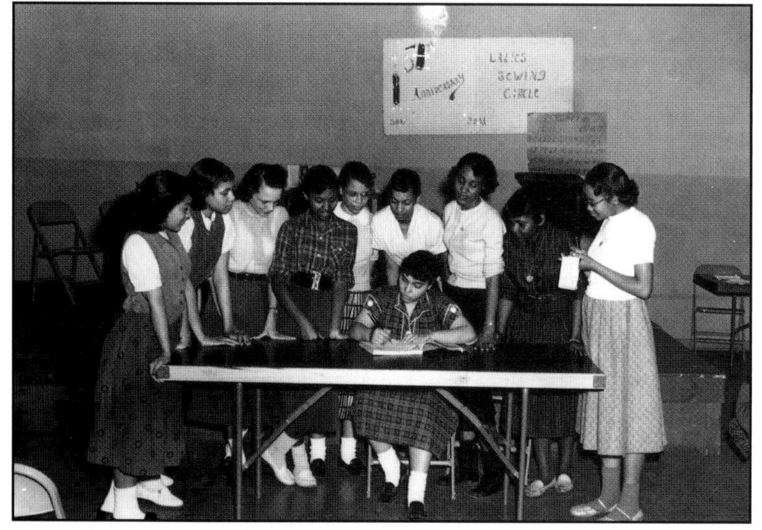

Teens at the T. N. Williams Center, 1950s.

Previous page: Students on the playground at Carver School.

"There will always be a Salem," Mayor James I. Moyer once remarked in response to an annexation threat to his town's existence. One wonders if founder James Simpson ever had the same thought.

Simpson had been dead for many a year, but his town still flourished. And really, not much had changed. Simpson saw opportunity in a dirt wagon road; later Salemites bet on an interstate highway. Simpson gambled that blacksmith shops and livery stables would bring prosperity; his descendants enthusiastically greeted the multimillion dollar General Electric plant. Simpson founded a town; 166 years later the town's citizens established a full-grown city. And on the 200th anniversary of Simpson's $20 real estate transaction with Susanna Cole, "Salem Pride" was on display.

The town greatly expanded her borders in her fourth half-century. In 1953, after much debate, South Salem was annexed, followed by the addition of an eastern tract in 1960. These additions confirmed Salem in the census of that year to be Virginia's largest town with a population of 16,058. A horseshoe of additional territory to the north, west and south was added in 1967.

Other changes marked the exciting decades of the 50s and 60s. The immense General Electric plant, constructed just outside of town in 1954, grew to employ over 2000 workers. Also in 1954, the T. N. Williams Community Center for African Americans opened on Water Street, providing the neigh-

Salem Civic Center, built 1967.

borhood with a meeting space, library, and heightened sense of community. In 1964, Interstate 81 reached Salem, bringing many more visitors to town and consequently new hotels and restaurants. 1967 saw the opening of the Salem Civic Center, replacing the Longwood mansion as a community center (which burned the following year).

Carver students in the 1960s. A generation later integrated students at Carver Elementary celebrate the school's 50th Anniversary with a maypole.

In tragedies far from home, four Salem men would give their lives in the Vietnam War, while countless others returned home to a changed world.

Along with the rest of the nation, Salem would in the 1960s experience the greatest change in race relations since Emancipation. The accelerating Civil Rights Movement pushed for integration of schools and public facilities. While other Virginia communities experienced massive resistance and great strife, Salem and Roanoke County desegregated schools easily, peacefully and ahead of schedule. The much revered Carver School became the integrated Salem Intermediate School for several years until alumni requests restored the old name.

"It wasn't planned that way," wrote Woody Middleton in the opening sentences of his epic history of Salem, "but 1967 was the year that Salem shucked off the old and pulled on the new. Down came the venerable Old Town Hall, up went the new Civic Center. Off came the

Historical Society President Sam Crockett looks on as a landmark plaque is placed on the Roanoke College Administration Building.

Pastor C. J. Smith and wife Irene (left) of First Baptist Church retire and are succeeded by James and Louise Braxton in 1968.

The new Salem High School, built 1977.

short pants, on went the long pants. 'We have grown up,' Mayor J. Leonard Shank said."

Shank was referring to perhaps the biggest transition in Salem's history: at midnight on January 1, 1968, Virginia's largest town became her newest independent city. In order to avoid the threat of annexation by the City of Roanoke, the town council had decided to seek independent status. The change was made quickly—and in relative secrecy, which inspired the criticism of some citizens and the admiration of others. Details of schools, services, and governance would occupy public discourse for years afterwards.

The new City of Salem faced innumerable challenges. Lingering questions of annexation suits and preservation issues sparked other debates. To protect Salem's historic character after the loss of several landmarks, the Save Old Salem Committee was formed in 1970. Concerned citizens identified historic structures worth preserving and worked to raise awareness of Salem's unappreciated heritage. After lapsing briefly in the mid-70s, the group was re-formed as the Salem Historical Society and has remained active in the community ever since.

A measure of the progress Salem had made in race relations came in April 1973. A group of African-American residents made an appeal to Salem City Council to change Water Street to Broad, the name used north of Main in the white neighborhood. The symbolism was important. Pastor James Braxton of First Baptist remarked that the change would "make blacks feel a part of the community. . ." and that "we want to become one with Salem." At issue then was not merely the names on the street signs, but rather the sense that when one crossed to the

The new Lewis-Gale Hospital in Salem, built 1972.

south of Main one entered a different community. After some debate, council agreed, and Water Street, the main black neighborhood for more than a century, disappeared from the map of Salem.

The city matured over the decades with the relocation of Lewis-Gale Hospital to town (1972), a new high school in west Salem (1977), a new city courthouse (1979), and a new post office (1982). West Salem Square Shopping Center and several modern hotels also appeared.

"Independent" was a word often used for modern Salem, which developed separate water and power systems. The much debated question of whether Salem should go it alone in public education was settled in 1983, when the century-old tie to Roanoke County was severed and Salem formed an independent school system. Salem schools quickly gained a reputation for superior education.

Downtown Salem was a topic of much debate. "The Hole"—a vacant lot at College and Main where Dillard's Drugstore had stood until 1965—was considered an unsightly eyesore, and an adult theater across the street an embarrassment. As part of a downtown revitalization effort, the City considered a proposal to turn Main Street into a pedestrian mall. The proposition never came to pass, perhaps in part because new shopping centers drew retail merchants out of downtown. Still, Salem persevered through her growing pains.

Dillard's Drugstore just prior to its destruction, and "The Hole" at College and Main.

One of the biggest challenges ever faced by Salem came in November 1985 with a disastrous flood. More than six and a half inches of rain fell in a 24 hour period, causing the Roanoke River to crest at an unprecedented 23 feet and every stream in the vicinity to overflow its banks. Damage in Salem was estimated at nearly $17 million. While no lives were lost in Salem, there were ten deaths in the Valley and 21 statewide.

Salem had always been a sports town, but that character was strongly reinforced in the 80s and 90s. A new Salem Stadium opened in 1985, and Salem High School football became even more of a local mania in the new home. Fans were rewarded with four state titles in five years under legendary coach Willis White (1996, 1998, 1999, and 2000). The Moyer Sports Complex, named for longtime mayor and judge James I. Moyer, was inaugurated in 1992, and in 1995, the $10 million, state-of-the-art Salem Memorial Baseball Stadium became the home field of the newly renamed Salem Avalanche Class A baseball franchise. In addition to the evident enthusiasm for local sports, the city achieved a national reputation as "Title Town," hosting the Stagg Bowl (Division III college national football title game) and numerous other sports championships. Thousands of amateur athletes set a goal of making it to Salem at the end of the season.

A Main Street landmark attracted much attention in 1987 as it inched through Longwood Park. The Williams-Brown House, built about 1845, had gone through several incarnations in its long life: home, store, frat house for Roanoke College, office space and, finally, vacant eyesore. When the home was threatened with destruction, the Salem Historical Society sprang into action. The owner offered the building to the Society, provided that the home be moved off site. The city donated an eastern corner of Longwood Park (where Poole's gas station had previ-

The way Salem might have been: the proposed Downtown Pedestrian Mall.

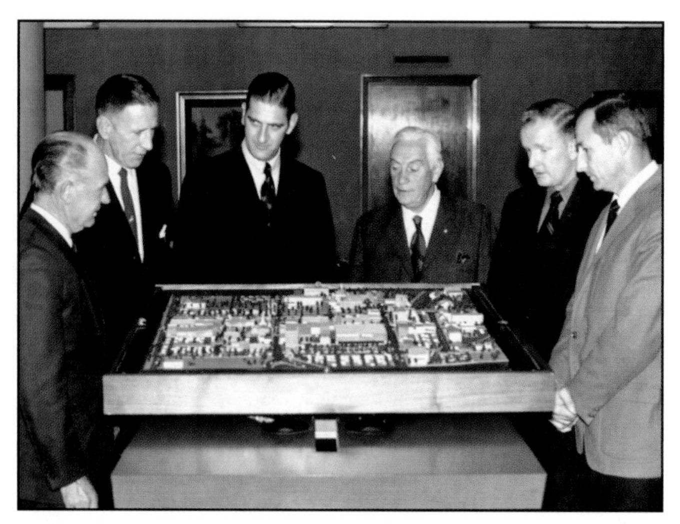

Officers of Farmer's National Bank examine a scale model of the revitalized downtown. Civic leader and bank president Ted Webber—Mr. Salem—is fourth from the left.

Aftermath of the 1985 Flood.

ously stood). After a whirlwind of fundraising, the house was moved up the hill. The relocation fulfilled a long-standing goal of the Historical Society: to create a local history museum. After extensive renovations, the Brown House opened as the Salem Museum in 1992.

The Williams-Brown House on the move, 1987.

Modern Salem had to learn to face new pressures. Land-locked and unlikely to annex more territory, questions of land use and preservation came to the forefront. A debate over whether to develop the old Elizabeth College campus, and to erect a new water tower there, was the centerpiece of the spirited 2000 city election. The incumbents all won, narrowly defeating several challengers, but first had to defend themselves against insinuations that the city government was unresponsive to citizens' input. Yet even the most vocal critics agreed that Salem was in the main well governed and was without a doubt a wonderful place to live. While there were issues to debate, there was more to celebrate.

And what better way to celebrate than a Bicentennial? Two centuries, twenty decades, 200 years, 2400 months, 10,400 weeks, more than 73,000 days. No matter how you divided it, by 2002 Salem had a lot of history to commemorate. After several years of planning, the city celebrated her Bicentennial with a year-long series of events, beginning with a costume ball in January and culminating with the Salem Museum's Holiday Homes Tour in December. The peak of the celebration came on May 25th with a Bicentennial Parade and a fes-

Opening of the Salem Museum 1992.

The Bicentennial Party in the Park, May 25, 2002.

tive Party in Longwood Park. At the Salem Museum, a special Bicentennial exhibit opened and a year-long time capsule project was inaugurated. That night, the Museum's Ghost Walk along Main Street introduced visitors to prominent figures from Salem's past, including Andrew Lewis, James Simpson and Susanna Cole.

"Friends, Family, Community" proclaimed the Bicentennial logo, a winning contest entry by Salem High student Ada Bamford. Without a doubt Salem values these three qualities. More commonly voiced, however, is the phrase "Salem Pride." Better than any others these two words embody the special spirit of the city as she enters her third century. Salem Pride means cheering throngs at every home football game; wide-eyed children at the Lake Spring Fishing Rodeo; city officials greeted on the street by first name; municipal services that don't cut corners; a fierce affection for all things Salem; and an immediate clarification for anyone who happens to confuse Salem with Roanoke.

"What makes Salem a great place to live today is what has made it a great place to live for 200 years. Its people," writes Delegate Morgan Griffith. "The forthrightness, grace, and simple dignity of its citizens that characterized our community when it was part of the American frontier remain its hallmark today.... As we celebrate our home's Bicentennial, I know that Salem's best days still lie ahead."

This love of home is perhaps more succinctly expressed by the fight song that Mayor Carl E. "Sonny" Tarpley is often known to quote: "I'm Salem born and Salem bred, and when I die, I'll be Salem dead."

Will there "always be a Salem"? As long as Salem Pride survives, bank on it. ❦

Mayor Sonny Tarpley, Vice Mayor Alex Brown, and their wives in the Bicentennial Parade.

Members of City Council, their wives, and city employees dressed in period costume for a special session of Council. Standing: Frank Turk, Gerald Pace, Jane and Howard Packett, Betty and Forest Jones, Mayor Sonny Tarpley and Joyce, Alex and Lisa Brown, John Givens, Joyce Bailey. Seated: Krystal Coleman, Melinda Payne, Patricia Givens.

The changing face of Main Street.

Rx
POWELL
Rexall
PHARMACY
Rx

"CUT INTO A GROWING
PROFESSION"
HAIR CUTTING & STYLING FOR MEN, WOMEN & CHILDRE
JOSEPH'S
HAIR CUTTING AND
COSMETOLOGY ACADEMY

The pressures of development became increasingly acute in the late 20th century, and with it came numerous debates over preservation. Like most communities, Salem lost some treasured buildings. Here are a few structures that were lost in this period.

Norman's Restaurant.

Intervale.

The Bank of Salem building on College Ave.

The Ordinary on Main Street.

The Old Town Hall at College and Clay.

The Windsor Motel on West Main.

Camp North near Salem offered African-American youth from as far away as New York City a chance to experience a summer in the mountains. It was run by the North Family from the 40s to the 70s.

The Salem passenger depot of the Norfolk and Western Railway was in operation from 1891 to 1965.

Hog slaughtering at the Baptist Orphanage.

Two of Salem's oldest institutions, the Baptist (middle) and Lutheran (bottom) Orphanages, faced numerous challenges in recent years. While orphans became thankfully more rare, the number of troubled youth and kids with special needs increased. Both institutions shifted their emphasis to ministering in these areas.

The third grade graduating class of Salem's North Cross School, 1958.

Carver High School had its share of championships. Number 11 is Wayne Harris, who later became the superintendent of Roanoke City schools.

The Andrew Lewis High Marching Band, 1963, and Cheerleaders, 1966.

Andrew Lewis won the state football championship in 1962.

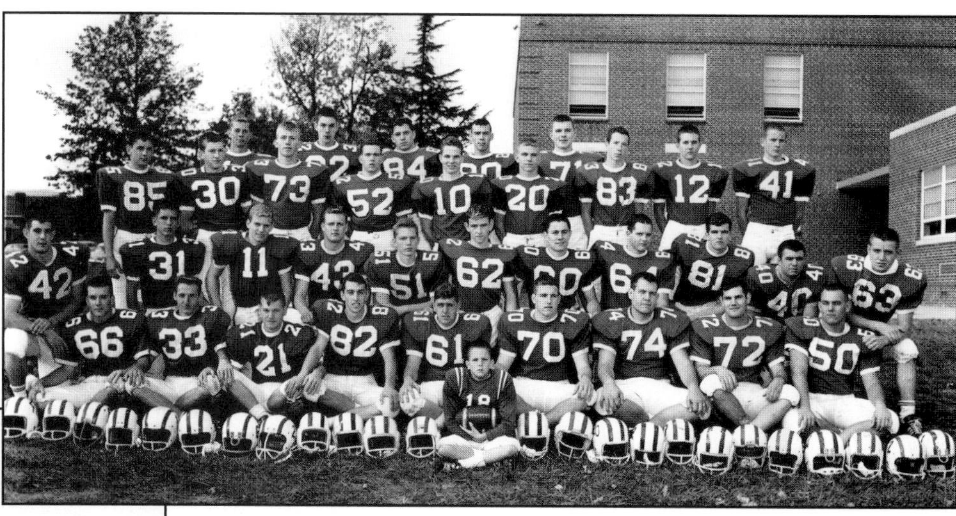

Fans enjoy a typical autumn Friday night in Salem.

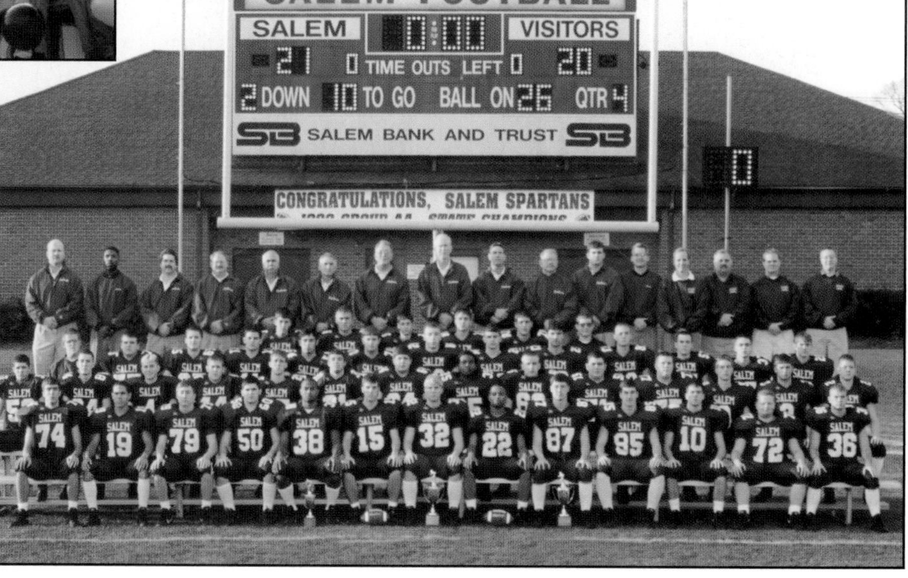

The 1999 Salem High Spartans won the state title with a 14-0 season.

Fans dance atop the dugout at a Salem Bucaneers baseball game.

Former mayor Leonard Shank (left) and then current mayor Jim Taliaferro throw out the first pitch at a 1992 Bucs game. Mayor Shank ably oversaw the transition from town to city status. But it was Mayor Taliaferro (served 1974-1996) who gave Salem its most notable features: a first rate independent school system, her reputation as a sports town with a top-flight baseball and football stadiums, and a fiercely proud "Salem first" attitude. "Jim Taliaferro made Salem what it is today," says City Manager Forest Jones.

Built in 1932, Municipal Field hosted Salem's high school sporting events into the 1980s and served as home field for a succession of professional minor league baseball teams until 1995.

Salem Memorial Stadium, a jewel of the Carolina League and home of the Avalanche, just after construction in 1995. Professional baseball has been a Salem summer pastime since the 1930s. Previous teams include the Wolves, Friends, Rebels, Pirates, Redbirds, and Buccaneers. Notice the pristine football field of Salem Stadium in the background.

These two aerial shots of downtown Salem (1967 and 1988) show two decades of growth.

The first Salem Library, built in 1937, was replaced in 1970 by a new building constructed on the same Main Street lot. At top left, the East family departs as the last patrons of the old library. At right, the library today.

Salem Police with teen auxiliary, 1969.

Construction of the new Salem City courthouse, 1979.

Fire at Holdren's on Main Street, February, 1979.

Salem Police Department "D" Platoon, 1975.

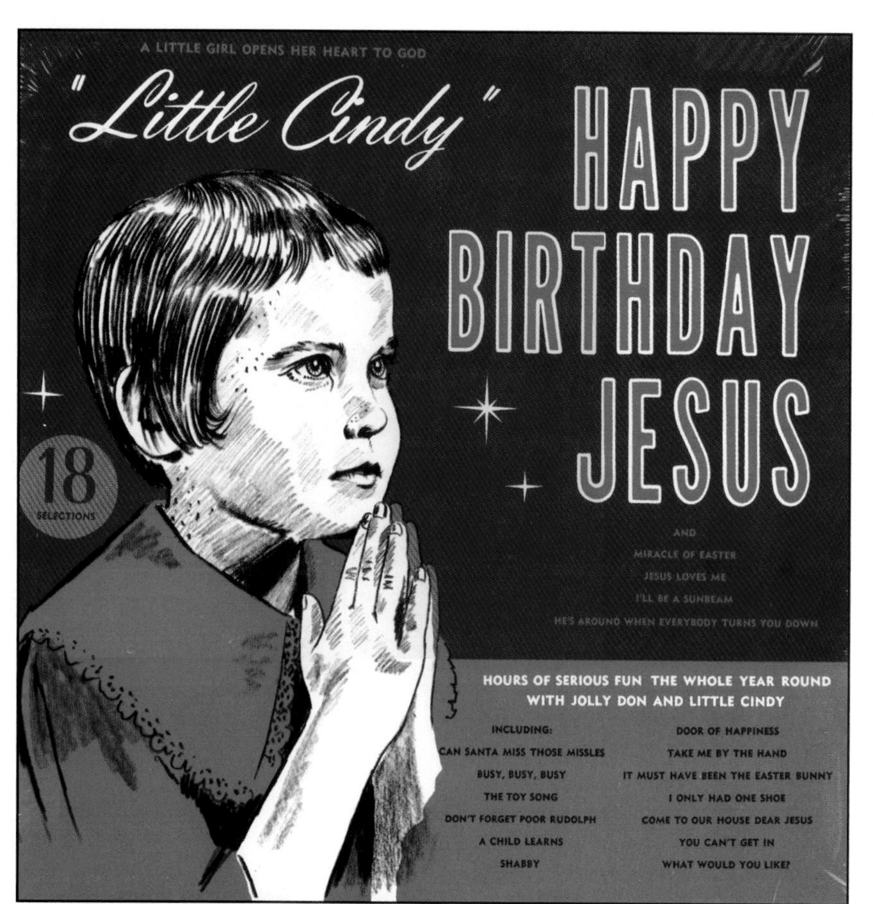

Don McGraw of Salem Records produced "Happy Birthday Jesus" by Little Cindy in 1964.

The Grievous Angels band of the 1970s.

1950s postcard.

Salem shared in America's Bicentennial celebrations in 1976. Here a group in front of the Salem Senior Center sports colorful colonial costumes.

1976 float of Independent Order of Odd Fellows.

ISH HATCHERY
VILLE, VIRGINIA

Salem enjoyed many beloved traditions in her fourth half-century: the first Fishing Rodeo at Lake Spring Park in 1960 (the Optimist Club, led by Bill Simmons, is stocking the lake); Art in the Alley; the Longwood Easter Egg Hunt; and parades for every occasion (here Cub Scouts take part in the Boy Scout Klondike Derby Parade, 1973).

Olde Salem Days, a beloved September tradition, fills Main Street with crafts, antique cars, and crowds of people.

The Salem Museum's Pauline Batten is ready to follow General Andrew Lewis, as she demonstrates frontier life in a bit of Olde Salem Days fun.

Dave Clark performs on Ridenhour Music's computer piano during Olde Salem Days.

Another annual tradition that caught on was the Salem Fair. From its humble beginnings in 1987, the fair soon became the second largest in the state, drawing tens of thousands of thrill seekers and filling a niche left by the demise of Lakeside.

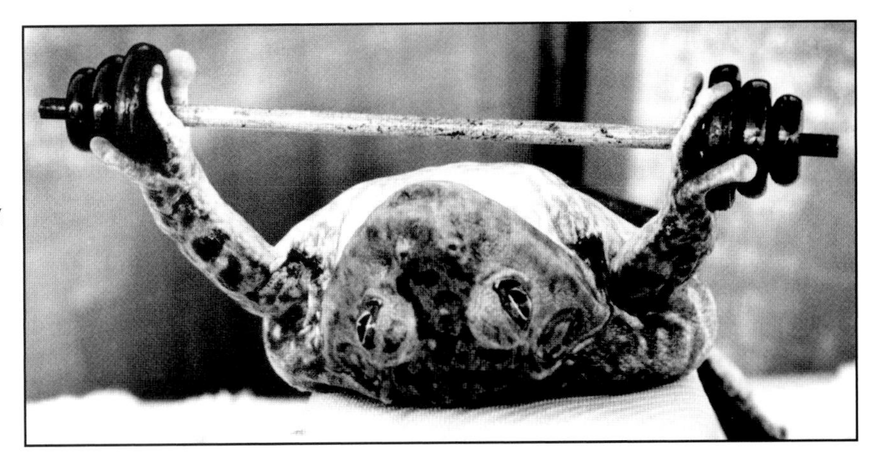

Photographer Tina Holtzlander captured this mesmerizing view of the fair's Ferris wheel.

The Roanoke Valley Horse Show traces its origins to 1972, although Salem hosted smaller versions going back to the 1930s. Held annually in June, the Horse Show became one of the most popular on the east coast.

Roanoke College history students reenact the 1066 Battle of Hastings.

One of the most lamented, and most remembered, images of the 1970s—Energy Crisis gas lines.

A scene that would have been perfectly natural in previous generations seems oddly anachronistic in 1979: Raymond Altizer's horse and buggy pass the old Academy Street School.

Among Salem's foremost photographers of the late twentieth century was Jonathan Fredin of the Salem Times-Register. *In addition to catching the news of the day, Fredin had an eye for capturing the beauty in everyday Salem scenes.*

HOWARD HOLLAND
FEB. 24, 1877

Photo Credits

All images used in this book are credited to the Salem Museum & Historical Society archives except as noted below. No image may be reproduced or transmitted in any form whatsoever without permission.

AAR = Abby Aldrich Rockefeller Folk Art Museum, Colonial Williamsburg
CLC = College Lutheran Church
C of S = City of Salem
HMWV = History Museum of Western Virginia
L of V = Library of Virginia
RC = Roanoke College
RT = Roanoke Times
STR = Salem Times-Register
VHS = Virginia Historical Society

13 sketch: Michele Moldenhauer, Archeological Society of Virginia
17 pistol: Dr. Richard Fisher
20 reenactment: Bron Duncan
24 valentine: Dorothy Butler
27 College and Bittle: RC; White: Wes McCarty
33 L of V
35 bottom: photo by Kevin Schweitzer
37-39: VHS
40-41: Sotheby's Auction House
44: L of V
46-47: AAR
57 bottom: CLC
60 bottom: STR
63 bottom: CLC
64 bottom: Mary F. Zimmerman
67 top: Chris Gladden
70 bottom: Rich and Patti Huggins
72 top: Bob Hunt; bottom left: Dorothy Butler
73 mill: Wes McCarty
74 top: Wes McCarty; bottom: Temp Norris
76 Fox: Shiloh Baptist Church
77 bottom: CLC
79 center and bottom: RC
80 bottom: Alex Brown
89-97: all RC
100 postcard: Bob Stauffer
101 bottom: Wes McCarty
102: Henry Bellinger
103 top: RC
104 bottom: RC
107: Mary F. Zimmerman
110 top: Bob Stauffer
111 Sam Good photo: Sam and Inez Good; all others: RC
112 top: Betty Clifton; bottom: Marie Dent
113: Marie Dent
114: Betty Hudson Brown
115 top: Betty Hudson Brown; bottom: Marie Dent
120-121: George Wade
122 top: George Wade; bottom: Bob Stauffer
124-126: Howard Birchfield
127 bottom: RT
128 top: Louise Hall; center: Nedra Crockett; bottom: Lellen Dawson
129 top: Jessie Graybill; center: Harriett Stokes; bottom: Ira and Judy Deyerle
130 top: Billy Branson; bottom: Dorothy Butler
131 top right: Henry Bellinger; Bottom: Harriett Stokes
132: Temp Norris
133 top: Mary Langhorne Clarke; bottom: C of S
138 bottom: George Wade
139 top: George Wade; bottom Edna Otey
140 bottom: Tootie Hildebrand
142-143: RC
144 top: Verda Williams; bottom: Mary F. Zimmerman
145 top: George Wade
146 bottom: RC
147 top: Moorman family
149 bottom: Aline Douglas
151: Bob Stauffer
158: C of S
159 bottom: C of S
160-161 all except Biggs portrait: Tootie Hildebrand
163 top: RC
164 bottom: Mrs. James P. Woods
165 top: Mr. and Mrs. James Gacek; bottom: Bob Hunt
167: Poindexter Bolt Advertising
168 top: HMWV; bottom: George Wade
169 center: HMWV; bottom: George Wade
171 inset: HMWV
174 top: George Wade; bottom: RT
175 top: STR; bottom: RT
176-183: all Poindexter Bolt Advertising
185: Marylen Harmon
186 top and center: HMWV
187 top and bottom: RT; center Marylen Harmon
188 center: Marylen Harmon
189 center and bottom: RT
190 bottom: RT
193 bottom: C of S
195 top: STR; bottom: RT
196 Norman's and Bank: RT
197 top: RT
198 top: Isabell and Henry Hylton
199 center and bottom: RT
200 top: Emily Carter; bottom: Marylen Harmon
201 top: Waneta Lawrence; bottom Emily Carter
202 top: Howard "Mooch" Semones; center: RT; bottom: Charlie Hammersley
203 top: RT; center and bottom: Brian Hoffman, STR
204: Brian Hoffman, STR
205: RT
206 top left: Judy East; others: RT
207 top and center: RT; bottom: C of S
208 bottom: Emily Carter
209 bottom: Waneta Lawrence
210 top: Jane Simmons; bottom: Harriet Stokes
211 top: STR; bottom: C. William Hill, Jr.
212 top: STR; bottom: RT
213 top and center: RT; bottom: Tina Holtzlander
214: RT
215 top: STR; bottom: RT
216-219: Jonathan Fredin

Index

JOHN D. LONG

John D. Long has taught history at Radford University, Virginia Western Community College, and is Senior Lecturer in History at Roanoke College. A *magna cum laude* graduate of Roanoke College, Mr. Long earned his Masters of Arts in History from the University of Virginia in 1991. As Curator/Educator for the Salem Museum, he has spearheaded a school outreach program, curated substantive historical exhibits, researched and written numerous articles for the *Historic Salem* newspaper, and initiated an innovative living history tour through Salem's cemeteries. He is the author of *South of Main: A History of the Water Street Community of Salem, Virginia* and winner of a 2002 Heritage Award from the Roanoke Valley Preservation Foundation.

MARY CROCKETT HILL

Mary Crockett Hill has served as Director of the Salem Museum & Historical Society since 1993. A Salem native, she graduated from Roanoke College and was a Henry Hoyns Fellow at the University of Virginia, where she studied Creative Writing. Ms. Hill's poetry has been published extensively in national journals, and her book *If You Return Home with Food* won the 1998 Bluestem Poetry Award. With Mr. Long, she received a 2002 Heritage Award from the Roanoke Valley Preservation Foundation. She lives with her husband Stewart and daughter Isabelle in a log home along the old Great Road.